Dreaming With God

Secrets to Redesigning Your World
Through God's Creative Flow

Dreaming With God

*Secrets to Redesigning Your World
Through God's Creative Flow*

BILL JOHNSON

DESTINY IMAGE® PUBLISHERS, INC.

P.O. Box 310, Shippensburg, PA 17257-0310

*"Speaking to the Purposes of God for this Generation
and for the Generations to Come."*

This book and all other Destiny Image, Revival Press, Mercy Place, Fresh Bread, Destiny Image Fiction, and Treasure House books are available at Christian bookstores and distributors worldwide.

For a U.S. bookstore nearest you, call 1-800-722-6774.
For more information on foreign distributors, call 717-532-3040.
Or reach us on the Internet: www.destinyimage.com

ISBN 10: 0-7684-2399-6
ISBN 13: 978-0-7684-2399-0

For Worldwide Distribution, Printed in the U.S.A.

2 3 4 5 6 7 8 9 10 11 / 09 08 07

Dedication

I dedicate this book to the "fathers" in my life. They lived unselfishly, seeing the best in me when I could see little of anything. They weren't always much older than me, but were always more mature and stable. I am forever indebted to them.

To my own dad, M. Earl Johnson. He lived at home as he did in the pulpit—honest, humble, visionary, devoted to his family, a man of character, great compassion, and lived life as a worshiper. He has gone home to be with Jesus, the lover of his soul. Thank you, dad! I am forever thankful for you.

To Chip Worthington. You taught me the value of the life of prayer and trained me to hunger for revival.

To Mario Murillo. You helped me to see that miracles are normal, revival is possible, and that being sold out to Jesus is the only acceptable way to live.

To Darol Blunt. You illustrated the life of grace, and helped me to discover the pleasure of the Lord over my life.

To Dick Joyce. Your commitment to me as a pastor of a small church in a small town established a standard of kingdom principles that I hope to never loose. You illustrated that the normal Christian life is a supernatural life.

To all of you, thank you. A million times, thank you.

Acknowledgements

My special thanks to Dann Farrelly, Carol Reginato, and Allison Armerding for your labor of love in editing my manuscript. This would have been near impossible without you.

To the whole Bethel Church family—you amaze me. Your tireless passion for God and your lifestyle of risk has helped to create the context for the greatest move of God I have ever witnessed. Together may we go to the next level!

Endorsements

Bill Johnson has an appetite for friendship with God, and all the mystery, revelation, power, and glory that comes with it. He can't bear to miss out. He contends for breakthrough, for the impossible, for all that only God can do. And in passion and worship he calls on God to allow us to experience what we thought was reserved only for the future. Bill is living in revival now, and it is a rare joy in this book to let him lead us to higher ground and increasingly taste the powers of the age to come.

Rolland Baker, Ph.D.
Heidi G. Baker, Ph.D.
Directors & Founders of Iris Ministries
Authors, *There's Always Enough*

Bill Johnson is a wonderful friend, a covenant brother, and a revivalist who is moving in extraordinary signs and wonders. He is also a mentor to me through his books and his revelatory teachings concerning the Kingdom of Heaven. I have no doubt that *Dreaming With God* will change your life as his teachings have impacted countless thousands.

Dr. Che Ahn
Senior Pastor Harvest Rock, Pasadena, CA
Founder and President of Harvest International Ministries
Author, *Into the Fire* and *Faith that Heals*

If you have ever wondered what God's ultimate intention and purpose is all about, you'll clearly discover the answer in Bill Johnson's newest book, *Dreaming With God*. When I read it I felt as if Bill was reading my thoughts and my yearnings. I felt like somebody finally had the guts to put these truths in printed form.

While Bill shares about the "tools" of the Kingdom trade as heirs of the Father, I believe this book is perhaps one of the greatest "tools" for accessing the riches of God's grace in the new millennium. When I think about Bill Johnson's life and ministry, one word emerges clear as crystal: Congruence. He embodies the quality and state of being in harmony both within and without. If you have ever heard any of his teachings, there is an ease of flow that is indicative of a life lived in harmony with the One who delights in intimacy with him. Take your time with each chapter and discover the secrets and the hidden mysteries of the indwelling Christ, apply your heart to wisdom, and dream big with God.

Mark J. Chironna, Ph.D
Mark Chironna Ministries
The Master's Touch International Church
Orlando, Florida

Bill Johnson's latest book, *Dreaming With God*, is written for Christian believers who are being "held in abeyance." It's not obeyance, it's abeyance. This is a military term describing the hand-picked soldiers a general trains for specialized activity, to win the war. The general keeps them on the sidelines and they are given special training that helps them achieve a readiness for the last battle. When the conflict reaches a certain stage that only the general recognizes, they are sent in fully prepared to win the war and carry it to finality.

While reading Bill's book I was impressed over and over again of his battle plan and how appropriate his explanations are for the final conflict between spiritual darkness and spiritual light. I believe this book is especially written for those of us now being held in abeyance. We're just waiting for our marching orders to get in and help wrap things up. You'll be spiritually challenged knowing you've been prepared for such a time as this.

Dick Mills
International Evangelist and Conference Speaker
Author, *The Spirit-Filled Believer's Daily Devotional*
and *Marriage Bliss*

Bill Johnson has made a major contribution in his latest book, *Dreaming With God*. It is a brilliant sequel to his previous two books.

The history of this era will record the awesome impact of Bill's thinking and writing. He has given us a report on the Kingdom of God, but that is not all. It is a report that is credible, balanced, authoritative, and laboratory proved. What is happening in Bethel Church in particular and Redding, California, in general, is confirming indeed. Add to this the fact that Bill is found dashing around the planet simply sharing the story and seeing the results of Kingdom preaching, and you have irrefutable evidence of the value of the message.

I asked Bill a few months ago, "What has the fact that you have been preaching the Kingdom message for 18 years have to do with what is happening right now in Bethel Church and Redding, California." His immediate and terse answer was, simply, "Everything!"

Jack Taylor
Founder of Dimensions Ministries
Author of *The Word of God With Power*

For the seeker, this book is a discovery of truths that will challenge the way you think and affect the way you live. It will require several readings to contain and apply the revelation found on every page. For me personally, it brought clarity to unspoken questions, practical understanding of my own desires and purpose, and passionate increase of love for my Father.

Karen Wheaton
Founder, The Ramp Youth Ministries
Recording Artist and TBN TV Host

Once again my friend, Bill Johnson, demonstrates a clarion call to bring Heaven down to earth. The content of this book is thought-provoking, inspiring, and most of all a clear challenge for Christians desiring to recapture their inheritance in God. Be advised: once you have read this book you will no longer be satisfied with the ordinary. Bill's passion to see the Kingdom of God established in our lives is highly contagious and will stir your appetite for extraordinary encounters with a supernatural God. Refreshing and real, this book will revolutionize your thinking.

Larry Randolph
International Conference Speaker
Author, *User Friendly Prophecy* and *Spirit Talk*

Writer Victor Hugo said, "There is nothing more powerful than an idea whose time has come." The truth is there is one thing more powerful, a God idea whose time has come. *Dreaming With God* is that idea.

Do you wish to live large in Christ in the greatest revival in history? Did you know you could be purpose-driven, talent-laden, and Spirit-powered? Did you know that the Church's destiny is not to impress the world by imitating the world? God has called us to overwhelm the world with original music, inventions, art, and miracles! Not only can we know God and worship God, we can *dream* with Him. This book shows you how to make those dreams a reality.

Original expression is virtually unlimited and as unique as every person God has created. Bill exposes the traditions that have limited

God and devastated our progress. Now we know why there have been so many casualties in spiritual warfare. We sent in only the preachers and told the rest of God's army to cheer us on from the sidelines as tithers.

This book hands out weapons to all the Christians. The arts, business, science, education, politics, and even the media are no longer a safe haven against a new breed of believer.

The common Christian can morph into a fountainhead of excellence, originality, and skills that will overwhelm this present darkness.

Mario Murillo, Evangelist
Founder, Mario Murillo Ministries
Author, *Critical Mass* and *I'm the Christian the Devil Warned You About*

Bill Johnson has captured one of the most important concepts in human development—how to dream the will of God. His inspiring and insightful presentation of the concept of "desire" and its role in human activity, creativity, wisdom, and personal fulfillment is guaranteed to provide answers to the deep questions of the human heart. I highly recommend this book and hope everyone will read it.

Dr. Myles Munroe
MMI - International
Nassau, Bahamas

Bill Johnson extends to us vital keys that will unlock the latent creativity residing in everyone who is willing to open their hands and take hold of the Kingdom purpose. Every chapter will take you through new thresholds leading you to greater appreciation of the uniqueness of your gifting.

Randall Worley
Founder, Headwaters Ministries
Apostolic Consultant and Conference Speaker

Bill Johnson's newest book, *Dreaming With God*, is great. Great because he has said things others were afraid to say because the statements were so contrary to traditional ways of interpreting Scripture or the traditional opinions of evangelical scholars.

Bill has written a book that is based in grace not law. It is about enjoying God as He enjoys us—not about performing for God. The author gets us to look at earth from Heaven's perspective, and to look at the Bible from a first-century perspective, instead of a 16th-century perspective. I doubt if anyone can read this without having to stop and think through the implications of its statements. *Dreaming With God* does not look at difficulties, challenges, or problems from earth's limitations, but from Heaven's unlimited power. This is not a book for the timid, the doubters, or those who want Christianity to be reduced to a mere moral philosophy. It is a book for those who desire the supernatural aspect of their Christian faith that is consistent with the Christianity of the Bible and the Christianity of the history of the Church that is full of the supernatural exploits of those who believe in Christ.

Randy Clark
Global Awakening Ministries
Author, *God Can Use Little ol' Me* and *There's More*

The *passion-driven worshiper* will always accomplish more than the *purpose-driven worker*. The first is motivated through friendship and intimacy, the latter through fear and responsibility. The Ephesian church was filled with those who persevered and toiled but had left their first love. Paul, on the other hand, commends those in Thessalonica for their labor of love.

Bill Johnson challenges us to rethink our priorities, thereby becoming *passionate partners* rather than *persevering producers*. After all it is those who *know* their God who will be strong and do exploits.

David Ravenhill
Author, *The Jesus Letters*
Lindale, Texas

I always cry when I read Bill Johnson's books. I cry because I am provoked to desire that has no language but tears. It's as if I am on the threshold of a kingdom that my spirit longs for and there is suddenly language and definition to concepts that have hitherto only rattled around in my spirit. As I read *Dreaming With God*, my spirit echoed the final words of the book: "The thought of missing something that could have been the experience of my generation is pure torture. I can't possibly sleep in this atmosphere, because if I do, I know I'll miss the reason for which I was born." *Dreaming With God* inspires me to live with God more deeply.

Stacey Campbell
Cofounder, Be A Hero
Coproducer and Coauthor, *Praying the Bible*

In Bill Johnson's book, *Dreaming With God*, Bill outdoes himself—as usual. In this new brilliant work, we're told that David, of the Bible, set a new "high water mark." But then, so does Bill Johnson. He tells us God is saying to each of us, "The Temple wasn't my idea. David was my idea." If you are, as this work states, one of those who feel "discouraged because their dreams have failed...," please know that Bill has written this book for *you*—because *you are God's idea*! And if that isn't good news, as they say, "it'll do until good news comes along!"

Steve Shultz
THE ELIJAH LIST
Founder, *The Voice of the Prophetic* magazine

The inspired Psalmist said, "the path of the just shines brighter till the perfect day." When the Church breaks through to new revelation, the whole world gets enlightened. The Reformation produced the Renaissance, and 90 percent of the world's inventions have been created since Azuza Street broke loose in 1906. As the Prophetic movement gathered momentum in the 1980s, another power surge occurred and knowledge began to double every seven years! Apostles are now bringing us into a rendezvous with "the perfect day" as men like Bill Johnson forge a path of revelation that is brighter with each book. As the world creeps into deeper darkness, torchbearers like Bill Johnson open portals to release the knowledge of the glory in language so tangible and accessible it can't help but inspire end-time exploits. It certainly inspires me!

Lance Wallnau
President, Lancelearning Group
International Conference Speaker

Contents

Foreword

Did you know that the stars speak?

They did in Abraham's day! The Creator of the universe gave a direct and amazing word to one of His friends. He told him to go out and count the number of stars that lit up the sky at night. Imagine, counting the stars at night!

So what did Abraham do? He went out and started counting the stars! I suppose it was something like this. Abraham goes out in the evening air after telling his wife, Sarah, good night and goes on a long walk pondering and peering into the heavens. He begins in obedience to count the stars while talking to himself and God. "One, two, four, twenty-seven, forty-five, one hundred fifty-five, two thousand sixty-two, ugh, ugh, ugh…Wow, count the stars?! What do you mean, I cannot count the number of stars—they seem so limitless."

The Lord replied, "Abraham—count the stars." Perplexed a bit as he attempts to mentally perceive what the man upstairs could mean by this strange command, Abraham continues in his quest to follow the direction of the unseen voice. "Three thousand seven hundred and…oh, I forgot—where was I?"

The voice is heard again, but this time offering some inside explanation. "The number of the stars will be the number of your descendants." "What, huh? Did you know that Sarah and I have been married for a long time and we don't have any fruit, let alone...?" But the voice of the Master persisted, "Count the stars. How many are there?"

Yes, the stars spoke to Abraham. Perhaps for a while, the voice of the stars haunted him as he would go out night after night staring into the realm of the impossible. But somewhere along the way, something changed. Did the circumstances change? No, well, not yet at least. What changed then? Abraham, like the rest of us, went from mentally assessing to heart believing.

Somehow God's dream seeped into Abraham's heart. After many trials and tests and errors, Abraham reached a point when he went out at night and he rejoiced when he looked up! "Yes, there's a promise! Yes, that one is for me! That star is declaring that God's Word will come true! In fact, that glimmering light right there is saying to me, the promises of God are 'Yes and Amen'!"

Yes, the stars do speak.

You know the rest of the story. It is a true-to-life piece of history that has effected us all. You see, God is a dreamer and He is looking for people who will dream His dreams with Him.

In every generation, dreamers arise. They think outside of man-made boxes and dare to forge ahead. But today a new breed of dreamers is arising. They not only talk of things to come—they call it into being in the here and now. They live their dreams.

Thus, I have the great pleasure and honor of introducing you to a man and a message. The man is Bill Johnson. His message is a dream for sure! It is with utmost esteem that I present to you an example of when a man and his message are one.

Behold, here comes another dreamer! Will you join the growing throng?

Yes, the stars continue to speak!

Wasted On Jesus,
James W. Goll
Cofounder of Encounters Network
Author, *The Lost Art of Intercession*, *The Seer* and *Dream Language*

Introduction

I write that His Church would rise to her potential and change the course of world history. We do not have an inferior message. It is the only one that can be demonstrated through the transformation of a life, family, and city. *Dreaming With God* is written in response to the cries of the devoted, but unfulfilled. It is to give true believers permission to dream, knowing that God longs for us to partner with Him in manifesting the divine plan.

Dreaming With God was the title of a chapter in my book, *The Supernatural Power of a Transformed Mind*. Don Milam, of Destiny Image Publishing, felt it deserved more attention than I was able to give it in one chapter. I agree, and have attempted to expand it in the following pages. Thank you, Don, for the encouragement.

CHAPTER 1

Co-laboring With God

God has made Himself vulnerable
to the desires of His people.

The disciples lived in awe of this One who called them to leave everything and follow. It was an easy choice. When He spoke, something came alive in them that they never knew existed. There was something in His voice that was worth living for—worth giving one's life for.

Everyday with Jesus was filled with a constant barrage of things they could not understand; whether it was a demoniac falling at Jesus' feet in worship, or the overbearing, religious leaders becoming silent in His presence; it was all overwhelming. Their lives had taken on a meaning and purpose that made everything else disappointing at best. Oh, they had their personal issues, for sure, but they had been apprehended by God and now nothing else mattered.

The momentum of the lifestyle they experienced would be hard for us to comprehend. Every word, every action seemed to have eternal significance. It must have occurred to them that to serve in the courts of this King would be far better than living in their own palaces. They were experiencing firsthand what David felt when he lived with God's presence as his priority.

THE ULTIMATE TRANSITION

Toward the end of His earthly life, Jesus gave His disciples the ultimate promotion. He told the twelve that He no longer called them servants, but friends. To be in the same room with Him, or even to admire Him from a distance, was more than they could have asked for. But Jesus brought them into His life. They had proven themselves worthy of the greatest promotion ever experienced by humanity—from servants to intimates. Perhaps only Esther of old could really understand what that exaltation felt like, as she, a servant girl who descended from captives, was promoted to queen. *"No longer do I call you servants, for a servant does not know what his master is doing; but I have called you friends, for all things that I heard from My Father I have made known to you"* (John 15:15). With this promotion, the disciples' attention would now shift from the task at hand to the One within reach. They were given access to the secrets in the heart of God.

When Jesus gave His disciples this promotion, He did so by describing the difference between the two positions. Servants don't know what their master is doing. They don't have access to the personal, intimate realm of their master. They are task-oriented. Obedience is their primary focus—and rightly so, for their lives depend on success in that area. But friends have a different focus. It almost sounds blasphemous to say that obedience is not the top concern for the friend, but it is true. Obedience will always be important, as the previous verse highlights, *"You are my friends if you do whatever I command you"* (John 15:14). But friends are less concerned about disobeying than they are about disappointing. The disciples' focus shifted from the commandments to the presence, from the assignment to the relationship, from "what I do for Him" to "how my choices affect Him." This bestowal of friendship made the revolution we continue to experience possible.

TRANSFORMED THROUGH PROMOTION

Several paradigm shifts take place in our hearts as we embrace this promotion. First, *what we know* changes, as we gain access to the heart of the Father. His heart is the greatest resource of information we need to function successfully in all of life. Jesus paid the price of our access to the Father, thereby granting us the *freedom* that comes from the truth we gain through that unlimited knowledge of His heart. Liberty is found in this phase of the promotion.

Second, our *experience* changes. Encounters with God as an intimate are quite different from those of a servant. His heartbeat becomes our heartbeat as we celebrate the shift in our own desires. The realm of His presence becomes our greatest inheritance, and divine encounters our greatest memories. Personal transformation is the only possible result from these supernatural experiences.

Third, our *function* in life radically changes. Instead of working *for* Him, we work *with* Him. We work not *for* His favor but *from* His favor. In this position He entrusts us with more of His power, and we are naturally changed into His likeness more and more.

Fourth, our *identity* is radically transformed. Our identity sets the tone for all we do and become. Christians who live out of who they really are cannot be crippled by the opinions of others. They don't work to fit into other people's expectations, but burn with the realization of who the Father says they are.

A SHIFT IN FOCUS

The classic example of the difference between servants and friends is found in the story of Mary and Martha. Mary chose to sit at Jesus' feet while Martha chose to work in the kitchen (see Luke 10:38-42).

Mary sought to please Him by being with Him while Martha tried to please Him through service. When Martha became jealous, she asked Jesus to tell Mary to help in the kitchen. Most servants want to degrade the role of the friend to feel justified in their works-oriented approach to God. Jesus' response is important to remember: "*Mary has chosen the better part.*" Martha was making sandwiches that Jesus never ordered. Doing more for God is the method servants use to increase in favor. A friend has a different focus entirely. They enjoy the favor they have and use it to spend time with their friend.

To say we need both Marys and Marthas is to miss the point entirely. And it simply isn't true. I've heard it said that nothing would ever get done if we didn't have Marthas. That, too, is a lie. That teaching comes mostly from servants who are intimidated by the lifestyle of friends. Mary wasn't a non-worker; she just learned to serve from His presence, only making the sandwiches that Jesus ordered. Working *from* His presence is better than working *for* His presence. Pastor Mike Bickle put it best when he said that *there are lovers and there are workers. And lovers get more work done than do workers!* A passionate lover will always outperform a good servant in pleasing Him.

THE WILL OF GOD

We usually think of the will of God as something static—fixed and unchangeable. We primarily associate it with specific events at certain times. The element missing in our understanding of this subject is our role in the unfolding of His will.

When God was going to destroy Israel, He told Moses to get out of the way, because He was going to kill the people that Moses had led out of Egypt into the wilderness. Moses then reminded God that they weren't his people—they were God's, and not only that, he didn't lead them out of Egypt, God did! God responded by basically acknowledging he was right, and then promised not to kill them.

The astonishing thing isn't so much that God changed His mind and spared Israel; rather, it was that He expected Moses to come into the counsel of His will, and Moses knew it. Abraham was another who understood this. These covenant friends throughout history all seemed to have a common awareness of God's expectation that they be involved in the demonstration of His will, influencing the outcome of a matter. They understood that the responsibility rested on their shoulders, and they must act before God to get what people needed. The priestly role of an intercessor was never more clearly illustrated. The primary focus of His will wasn't whether or not to destroy Israel; it was to bring Moses in on the process. His will is not always focused on events; it is focused on His friends drawing near into His presence, standing in their roles as delegated ones. The will of God is as much process as it is outcome—often fluid, not static.

THE BLANK CHECK

As kids, many of us dreamed about being granted one wish. Solomon got the "one wish." When God appeared to Solomon and gave him that opportunity, it forever raised the bar of our expectations in prayer. The disciples were given the same "wish," only better. Instead of one blank check, they were given an unlimited supply of blank checks. And this gift was specifically granted in the context of their friendship with God.

Surrounding their promotion to friendship, Jesus gave His disciples this amazing list of promises. Each promise was a blank check they were to live by and use throughout their lives for the expansion of the Kingdom. They are as follows:

*If you abide in Me, and My words abide in you, you will **ask what you desire**, and it shall be done for you* (John 15:7).

You did not choose Me, but I chose you and appointed you that you should go and bear fruit, and that your fruit should *remain, that **whatever you ask** the Father in My name He may give you* (John 15:16).

***If you ask anything** in My name, I will do it* (John 14:14).

*And in that day you will ask Me nothing. Most assuredly, I say to you, **whatever you ask the Father** in My name He will give you. Until now you have asked nothing in My name. **Ask, and you will receive**, that your joy may be full* (John 16:23-24).

For us to properly receive what Jesus has offered us in these verses, any robotic understanding of what it means to be a follower of God has to change. God never intended that the believer be a puppet on a string. God actually makes Himself vulnerable to the desires of His people. In fact, it can be said, "if it matters to you, it matters to Him."

While much of the Church is waiting for the next word from God, He is waiting to hear the dream of His people. He longs for us to take our role, not because He needs us, but because He loves us.

FAMILY REUNION

My mother's side of the family had a family reunion in the early '90s. Around 160 people came from all over the world to the campground we rented in northern California. Astonishingly, they represented 48 different pastors and missionaries.

It had to be one of the most highly unusual reunions on record because of the extraordinary number of ministers involved. But it was even more unique because it was so much like a formal conference. There were meetings, panel discussions, and the like. I was even asked to write a song for the event, taken from the Old Testament Book of Zephaniah. It was a great time of celebrating the grace of God upon our family.

On one of the evenings, someone had scheduled a square dance as a recreational activity. Now, I don't dance, except in worship. It doesn't matter to me if it's square dancing, or if it's on some night-club dance floor, I simply don't dance. I find it to be an embarrassing activity. In junior high, I got out of square dancing by telling the teacher that my church didn't believe in it (which was partially true). And here at this reunion, this embarrassing behavior was scheduled as a family activity. Wonderful!

When Beni, my wife, asked what I was going to do, I told her emphatically: "I don't dance!" She already knew my thoughts and wisely chose to not attempt the impossible, which was to talk me out of such an idea so that I could join in the family fun. (One of the strengths of my personal makeup is that I don't change my mind easily. It doesn't matter who is challenging my position. I just don't move. One of the weaknesses of my personal makeup is that I don't change my mind easily.)

We went to the hall where the party was in full swing, as entire families were attempting to dance together. It was fun to watch. It was also obvious which families actually knew what they were doing, and which ones didn't. We laughed and watched as people stepped on each other's feet, awkwardly attempting to learn such difficult moves so quickly. Then the unexpected happened. My daughter, Leah, then about 10 years old, asked me if I would dance with her.

I am known for being unmovable. Some family members call it stubborn; I call it commitment. Yet in that moment I felt like I had been ambushed. My feet were solid, my resolve firm, and my argument was steadfast. But daughters, especially 10-year-old daughters, have a way of getting in under the radar. To my horror, I found myself without a will saying, "Yes." Where was my toughness? What about my resolve? Where did my gift of stubbornness go when I needed it most? To this day I don't know. I had been "brought to my knees" by a little girl. Moments later I was on the dance floor, attempting what I knew better than to attempt. But the look in my little girl's eyes told me all was well. Her pleasure more than made up for my embarrassment. And I understood again how fathers willingly make themselves vulnerable to the desires of their children—and how God joyfully makes Himself vulnerable to the desires of His people.

GOD'S SOVEREIGNTY

There is no question that spending time with God changes our desires. We always become like the one we worship. But it's not because we've been programmed to wish for the things He wants us to wish for; it's because in friendship we discover the things that please Him—the secret things of His heart. It is the instinct of the true believer to search for and find, that which brings pleasure to the Father. Our nature actually changes at conversion. It is our new nature to seek to know God and to please Him with our thoughts, ambitions, and desires.

Those who have the greatest difficulty with this line of thinking are those who consider this to be an assault on the doctrine of the sovereignty of God. There is no question; God is sovereign. But His position of rulership is not denied by our assignment to co-labor with Christ. One of my favorite quotes on this subject comes from my dear friend Jack Taylor. He says, *"God is so secure in His sovereignty that He is not afraid to appear un-sovereign."*

ALL DESIRE HAS A FATHER

A good way to remember the intent of the word *desire* is to break it down by syllables. "De" means "of." And "sire" means "father." All desire is "of the father." The question should not be, "are my desires from God?" The question should be, "With what, or with whom have I been in communion?"[1] I can commune with God or with the enemy. If I take time to ponder an offense I experienced some years ago, and I begin to wonder if God ever judged that person, the desires of vindication and retaliation will stir up in my heart.

Why? Because I have been fellowshipping with the *father* of bitterness, and those desires are the *children* formed in my heart.

If fellowshipping with evil can produce evil desires in us, how much more should it be said that time with God forms desires in us that have eternity in mind and ultimately bring Him glory? The thing to note is this: these desires are not there by command; they are in our hearts because of our fellowship with God. They are the offspring of our relationship with Him.

The main purpose of this book is to teach and encourage believers to live from the desires that are born in them through their intimate fellowship with the Lord. Many believers discount their desires, automatically trying to get rid of everything they want in order to prove their surrender to God. Their selfless approach overshoots the will of God and actually denies the fact that God is the Father of the dreams and abilities within them. It sounds good on the outside because of its selfless religious appeal, but it works against God's purposes on the inside. Most still don't see the difference between the entrance *to* the Kingdom, and life *in* the Kingdom. We enter on a straight and narrow road, saying, *"Not my will but Yours be done."* The only door is Christ Jesus. The only way to find life in Christ is to come in complete abandonment to Him.

But life in the Kingdom, which is past the narrow entrance of salvation, is completely different. It's bigger on the inside than it is on the outside. It is here we find the Lord saying to us that we're no longer servants, but friends. It's in that context He says that the Father will give us whatever we want. The emphasis is on *what you want*. Granted, we can't forget the context, or we'll just create more selfish people who confess Christ. Just as the Cross precedes the resurrection, so our abandonment to *His will* precedes God attending to *ours*. But the opposite emphasis also has dangers—if we never become people of desire, we will never accurately and effectively represent Christ on the earth.

THE TREE OF LIFE

"*...desire fulfilled is a tree of life*" (Proverbs 13:12 NASB). Solomon gave us this amazing statement. If there was anyone qualified to discuss *fulfilled personal desires* it was Solomon. In Second Chronicles 7:11, it says, "*Solomon successfully accomplished all that came into his heart....*" We can't allow his disobedience later in life to deter us from the profound lessons learned through his obedience early in life. He experienced the power of having his heartfelt desires accomplished.

Solomon's words revisit the subject of the tree of life found in Genesis. It connected Adam and Eve to eternity. (After eating the forbidden fruit, the angel of the Lord guarded the way to the tree of life so that Adam and Eve could not eat its fruit; it made eternal whatever it touched. It would make their sinful condition permanent—an eternal, unredeemable state.) Here we are told that a believer will experience the tree of life as their desires are fulfilled. This implies that those who taste the wonder of fulfilled desires in Christ will be given eternal perspective and identity through that fulfillment. The process of surrender, personal transformation, and fulfilled desires is the training ground for reigning with Christ forever.

In John 16:24, it says that God wants to answer our desires (prayers), "*...that your joy may be full.*" No wonder there's been so little joy in the church. Joy is the result of our redeemed heart reveling in its participation in God's unfolding plan for the earth through prayer. More specifically, joy comes through having our prayers answered.

Answered prayers, especially those that require supernatural intervention, make us happy! And happy people are fun to be with. Perhaps that's why Jesus was called the friend of sinners (see Luke 7:34). His joy exceeded all those around Him. Moment by moment, day after day, He saw His prayers answered by His heavenly Father. His joy was what many would consider extreme. In Luke 10:21, it says, "*Jesus rejoiced in the Spirit.*" The word *rejoiced* in that context suggests "shouting and leaping with joy."[2] Even proximity to Jesus brought joy.

John the Baptist leapt for joy in his mother's womb because Mary, who was pregnant with Jesus, entered the room. Jesus' joy is contagious, and must become the mark of true believers once again.

DAVID SETS A NEW "HIGH WATER MARK"

An extraordinary example of fulfilled dreams is illustrated in Solomon's building of a temple that his father, David, had planned. The building and consecration of Solomon's temple is one of the most significant events in the Bible. Yet at the temple's dedication, Solomon said,

> *Blessed be the Lord God of Israel, who spoke with His mouth to my father David, and with His hand has fulfilled it, saying, 'Since the day that I brought My people Israel out of Egypt, I have chosen no city from any tribe of Israel in which to build a house, that My name might be there; but I chose David to be over My people Israel.' Now it was in the heart of my father David to build a temple for the name of the Lord God of Israel* (1 Kings 8:15-17).

God said that He didn't choose a city, He chose a man, and the idea for a temple was in the heart of the man. God basically said: The temple wasn't my idea. *David* was my idea. Incredible! David's creativity and desires helped write history because God embraced them. David gave us many Kingdom principles, which set the direction in which we are to live. It is as if he said, "Dreamers! Come! Let's dream together and write the story of human history." You are God's idea, and He longs to see the treasure that is in your heart. As we learn to dream with God we become co-laborers with Him.

ADAM—THE FIRST CO-LABORER

God assigned Adam the task of naming all the animals (see Gen. 2:19). Names had much richer meaning in those days because they represented the nature of something. I believe that Adam was actually assigning to each animal its nature, its realm of authority, and the dimension of glory it would enjoy. In reality, Adam's assignment was to help define the nature of the world he was to live in. This co-laboring role was a creative role, complimentary to God the Creator. God brings us into these situations, not because He can't do it Himself. He delights in seeing all that He made come into its identity in Him by embracing its divine purpose. To embrace the privilege of creative expression is consistent with being made in the image and likeness of our Creator.

THE TOOL THAT SHAPES HISTORY

The King James Bible highlights the role of our desires in the way it translates Mark 11:24, "*Therefore I say unto you, what things soever ye desire, when ye pray, believe that ye receive them, and ye shall have them.*" We are to pay attention to our desires *while we're enjoying the presence of God in prayer*. Something happens in our time of communion with Him that brings life to our capacity to dream and desire. Our minds become renewed through divine encounter, making it the perfect canvas for Him to paint on. We become co-laborers with Him in the master plan for planet earth. Our dreams are not independent from God, but instead exist *because of* God. He lays out the agenda—*On earth as it is in Heaven*—and then releases us to run with it and make it happen! As we grow in intimacy with Him, more of what happens in life is a result of our desires, not simply receiving and obeying specific commands from Heaven. God loves to build on our wishes and desires, as He embraced David's desire for the temple.

This truth is risky from our perspective because we see those who live independent of God and only want Him to validate their dreams. True grace always creates a place for those with evil in their heart to come to the surface through increased opportunity. But the richness of this truth is worth pursuing in spite of the perceived danger, because only this truth enables the Church to come fully into her destiny through co-laboring with the Lord.

This divine destiny was announced by the Psalmist long before the blood of Jesus made it a possible lifestyle. *"Delight yourself also in the Lord, and He shall give you the desires of your heart"* (Psalms 37:4).

DREAMERS WELCOME HERE

We were born to create, to build, and to advance. This requires an ongoing display of supernatural wisdom to succeed. Wisdom, and its unique expression, is the focus of the next chapter.

ENDNOTES

1. Quotes from Lance Wallnau.
2. Footnote in the Spirit-Filled Life Bible.

Chapter 2

The Creative Edge

When unbelievers lead the way in inventions
and artistic expression, it is because the
church has embraced a false kind of spirituality.

One of the most natural parts of being created in the image of God is the ability to dream. It's a God-given gift. Yet many believers, in their attempts to please God, kill the very capacity He gave them. They reason, "To really please God I must get rid of everything to do with self!" It sounds spiritual to many, but it's more Buddhist than Christian. If we pursue that line of thinking for long we end up with neutered believers. Self-mutilation need not be physical to be a perversion. Anytime we try to cut away at what God placed in us, we are entering a form of spirituality that the Scriptures do not support, and are contributing to a spirit that works against us having a truly effective witness. It is not wise to crucify the resurrected man and call it discipleship. The Cross is not for the new man; it's for the old man (Romans 6:5-9).

Many have even prayed, "None of me, all of You." God had none of us before we were born and didn't like it. He created us for His pleasure. A better prayer would be, "All of me covered by all of

You!" Even John the Baptist's statement, "He must increase but I must decrease" is often misapplied in order to endorse the self-depreciating form of Christianity. Look at the context; he was passing the baton to Jesus. His job was to prepare the way for the Messiah. It was important for him to be out of the way, as he closed out the Old Testament prophetic ministry. Jesus would bring about the fulfillment of all the prophets had announced and initiate God's manifest dominion on the planet. John the Baptist passed the baton to Jesus, who has passed it on to us *that we might increase.*

This confusion over our value and identity is sometimes most acute in revival, as the outpouring of the Spirit always brings an increased awareness of our sinfulness. Some of the greatest hymns of confession and contrition have been written during such seasons. But the revelation of our sin and unworthiness is only half of the equation. Most revivals don't get past this one point, and therefore cannot sustain a move of God until it becomes a lifestyle. It's difficult to build something substantial on a negative. The other half of the equation is how *holy* He is on our behalf and who we are as a result. When this is realized, our identity changes as we embrace the purpose of our salvation by faith. At some point we must go beyond being simply "sinners saved by grace." As we learn to live from our position in Christ, we will bring forth the greatest exploits of all time.

Throughout much of church history people have been stripped of their God-given gifts, talents, and desires, under the guise of *devotion to Christ.* This stripped-down version of Christianity removes the believer from ministry, and relegates that privilege to a certain class of Christian called "ministers." The regular believer's role is reduced to financial and emotional support of those in public ministry. To work without fulfilled dreams and desires is to partner with the religious spirit that exalts routine without purpose, and calls it suffering. The honor of giving to promote ministry must not be devalued, but its emphasis should never be at the expense of each individual carrying their own creative expression of the Gospel through realizing their God-given dreams and desires.

Like Father, Like Son and Daughter

Our heavenly Father is the Creator of all, and the Giver of all good gifts. His children should bear His likeness, which means they should be creative. When unbelievers lead the way in inventions and artistic expressions, it is because the church has embraced a false kind of spirituality. It is not living in a true Kingdom mentality, which is the renewed mind.[1] The renewed mind understands that the King's dominion must be realized in all levels of society for an effective witness to take place. Someone with a Kingdom mind-set looks to the overwhelming needs of the world and says, "God has a solution for this problem. And I have legal access to His realm of mystery. Therefore I will seek Him for the answer!" With a Kingdom perspective, we become the answer in much the same way Joseph and Daniel were to the kings of their day.

To be free to dream with God, one must learn to be a co-laborer. The desire of the true believer is never independence from God. The goal is not to find ways to shape God's thinking, as though He were in need of our input. Instead it is to represent Him well. Learning to display His heart instinctively and accurately is the passion of true lovers of God. His heart is to redeem all people, and the tools He uses to display His goodness are gloriously vast, reaching into the heartfelt needs of every individual. Only divine wisdom can meet that challenge.

Learning the dreams of God for this world is our beginning place. Dreaming can be expensive. We know that the Father's dream of redeeming humanity cost Him the life of His Son. However, partnering with Him in His dreams will release in us a new capacity to dream like Him.

WISDOM CREATES

Wisdom and creativity are related subjects in the Bible. In fact, creativity is a manifestation of wisdom in the context of excellence and integrity. Wisdom is personified in Proverbs 8, and is the companion of God at the creation of all things. Therefore wisdom and creativity must not be separated in the mind of the believer. They are the essential tools needed to complete our assignment of being an effective witness to the lost. It is wisdom that makes our role in this world desirable to them. While most Christians have a value for wisdom, most do not have an equal value for the role of creativity in their God-given responsibilities. Yet it is creativity that illustrates the presence of wisdom: "*Wisdom is vindicated by all her children*" (Luke 7:35 NASB).

The six days of creation saw the most wonderful display of wisdom and art imaginable. As God spoke, the worlds were made. Light and beauty, sound and color, all flowed together seamlessly as wisdom set the boundaries for creation itself. Solomon, the man known for supernatural wisdom, discusses the co-laboring effect that wisdom had on that day:

> *When He marked out the foundations of the earth; Then I was beside Him, as a master workman; and I was daily His delight, rejoicing always before Him, rejoicing in the world, His earth, and having my delight in the sons of men* (Proverbs 8:29-31 NASB).

Wisdom is given an artisan title of "master workman." Note the even more powerful phrases; "*rejoicing always before Him,*" "*rejoicing in the world,*" and "*my delight in the sons of men.*" Wisdom is not stoic as it is so often pictured. It's even more than happy; it is celebratory in nature and finds pleasure in the act of creation. But its greatest delight is in us! It has found perfect companionship with humanity. We were born to partner with wisdom—to live in it and display it through creative expression.

WISDOM, THE MASTER CRAFTSMAN

The first mention of a person filled with the Holy Spirit in Scripture was Bezalel. He was called upon to head up a building project for Moses. His assignment was to build God a house that He might dwell among His people. God revealed what He wanted that house to look like, but it would take a special gift of wisdom to know "how" to get it done. That is where Bezalel came into the picture. He was given supernatural wisdom to complete the task with artistic excellence. It was wisdom that qualified him to take on this assignment, and it was wisdom that enabled him as an artisan or master craftsman to design and build what was in God's heart.

Notice the bold print in the following verses. It is the cause and effect of being filled with His Holy Spirit:

*I have **filled him with the Spirit of God** in **wisdom**, in understanding, in knowledge, and in all kinds of **craftsmanship**, to make **artistic designs** for work in gold, in silver, and in bronze, and in the cutting of stones for settings, and in the carving of wood, that he may work in all kinds of **craftsmanship** (Exodus 31:3-5 NASB).*

*Then Moses said to the sons of Israel, "See, the Lord has called by name Bezalel the son of Uri, the son of Hur, of the tribe of Judah. And He has **filled him with the Spirit of God,** in **wisdom,** in understanding and in knowledge and in all **craftsmanship**; to **make designs** for working in gold and in silver and in bronze, and in the cutting of stones for settings and in the carving of wood, so as to perform in every **inventive work.** He also has put in his heart to teach, both he and Oholiab, the son of Ahisamach, of the tribe of Dan. He has filled them with **skill to perform every work** of an engraver and of a designer and of an embroiderer, in blue and in purple and in scarlet material, and in fine linen, and of a weaver, as **performers of*** *every work and makers of designs* (Exodus 35:30-35 NASB).

Artistic design, excellence, and *inventive work* are a few of the characteristics of wisdom in this passage. That is part of what being filled with the Spirit looked like in Moses' day. The New Testament adds the power element, because every believer now has access to the miracle realm through the outpouring of the Holy Spirit. This new emphasis does not abolish the original revelation of the subject, but uses it as a foundation to build upon. If we combine the two we end up with believers who walk in wisdom, making practical contributions to the needs of society, who also confront the impossibilities of life through the provisions of the Cross, bringing solutions through supernatural display of miracles, signs, and wonders. Perhaps it is these two things working in tandem that should be considered *the balanced Christian life.*

THE WAR OF ART

Then I lifted up my eyes and looked, and behold, there were four horns. So I said to the angel who was speaking with me, "What are these?" And he answered me, "These are the horns which have scattered Judah, Israel and Jerusalem." Then the Lord showed me four craftsmen. I said, "What are these coming to do?" And he said, "These are the horns which have scattered Judah so that no man lifts up his head; but these craftsmen have come to terrify them, to throw down the horns of the nations who have lifted up their horns against the land of Judah in order to scatter it (Zechariah 1:18-21 NASB).

This is one of the more alarming passages in the Bible. Not because it deals with spiritual warfare, but because God's tools for victory are not common knowledge for most of us today.

In these verses the people of God are being terrorized and scattered by abusive authorities and powers (horns). Hopelessness is the theme of the day, and the confidence that God is with them is at an all time low. The God of all wisdom illumines a truth that is to awaken the people of God to His end-time plans. He sends forth His army to tear down the military strongholds. Who are His soldiers? Craftsmen! Not since God first sent a choir into war[2] has there been such an outlandish strategy for battle. This is a plan that only Wisdom could design.

When creativity is the normal expression of God's people there is something that happens to all who oppose Him. They become disheartened. The devil himself has no creative abilities whatsoever. All he can do is distort and deform what God has made. God is made known through His works. When His works flow through His children their identity is revealed, and there is an inescapable revelation of the nature of God in the land. He is irresistible to those who have eyes to see.

The four craftsmen were God's answer to the four horns that had attempted to scatter His people. Those committed to skillful wisdom (artistic expression) will dismantle the strongholds of abusive power. Not only will they overcome them in a military sense, they will terrify supernatural and counterfeit powers to their core! This is the mission and outcome for entering God's Last Days strategy of infiltrating the world system with skillful wisdom—wisdom from above.

Craftsmen are not simply woodworkers and painters. Nor does that title belong only to actors and musicians. Everyone, doing their God-given task with *excellence, creativity,* and *integrity* is a craftsman in the biblical sense. Schoolteachers, businessmen and women, doctors and lawyers, and all those who have surrendered their gifts to the purposes of God need to display divine wisdom. The opposition that surrounds us seems great, but it cannot stand against the demonstration of God's people wielding this great weapon of war. From the housewife to the brain surgeon, from the preacher to the professor, all must be filled with the Spirit of God until we are known for wisdom, turning the heads of the *queens of Sheba* once again (see 1 Kings 10:1-10). She traveled a great distance just to see extraordinary wisdom. The Bible tells us that in the last days the nations will come to His holy nation asking us to teach them the Word of the Lord (see Micah 4:1-2). Is it possible that this is their response to seeing us filled with the Spirit until His wisdom is on display? I think so.

THE NATURE OF WISDOM

The world's definition of wisdom is focused on the attainment and use of knowledge. It's not wrong; it's just misleading. The church has adopted their incomplete definition, pursuing a wisdom that has no soul. Biblical wisdom sees with divine perspective, and is the creative expression of God, bringing practical solutions to the issues of everyday life.

Besides Jesus, Solomon was the wisest man to ever live. He caught the attention of his entire generation. People were in awe of his gift. The royalty in other nations envied his servants who had the privilege of being exposed to his gift on a daily basis. *A servant in the presence of wisdom is better off than being a king without wisdom.* The queen of Sheba was stunned by how wisdom affected simple things like clothing, buildings, and the like. Examine her perspective:

> *And when the queen of Sheba had seen the wisdom of Solomon, the house which he had built, the food at his table, the seating of his servants, the attendance of his ministers and their attire, his cupbearers and their attire, and his stairway by which he went up to the house of the Lord, she was breathless* (2 Chronicles 9:3-4 NASB).

The effects of his gifts brought Israel into the greatest time of peace and prosperity they had ever known. Wisdom, through one man, changed a nation. What could happen with millions embracing this God-given opportunity?

The wisdom of God will again be reflected in His people. The Church, which is presently despised, will again be reverenced and admired. The Church will again be a *praise in the earth* (see Jer. 33:9).

The manifestations of wisdom are varied. But as mentioned earlier, its nature can be seen in three words—integrity, creativity, and excellence. Divine wisdom springs from *integrity*, and becomes manifest through *creative* expression with *excellence* as its standard. Wherever we find ourselves operating in any of these three expressions we are being touched by divine wisdom.

Let's examine the three characteristics of divine wisdom:[3]

Integrity – a) Adherence to moral and ethical principles; soundness of moral character; honesty. b) The state of being whole, entire, or undiminished. c) A sound, unimpaired, or perfect condition. *Synonyms* – honesty, truth, truthfulness, honor, veracity, reliability, and uprightness.

Integrity is the expression of God's character revealed in us; and that character is the beauty of His perfection—His holiness. Holiness is the essence of His nature. It is not something He does or doesn't do. It is who He is. It is the same for us. We are holy because the nature of God is in us. It begins with a heart separated unto God and becomes evident in the Christ-nature expressed through us.

Creativity – a) The state or quality of being creative. b) The ability to transcend traditional ideas, rules, patterns, relationships, or the like, and to create meaningful new ideas, forms, methods, interpretations, etc.; originality, progressiveness, or imagination. c) The process by which one utilizes creative ability. *Synonyms* – originality, imagination, inspiration, ingenuity, inventiveness, resourcefulness, creativeness, and vision.

Creativity will not only be seen in a full restoration of the arts; it is the nature of His people, expressed in finding new and better ways to do things in any area of influence. It is a shame for the Church to fall into the rut of predictability and call it "tradition."

We must reveal who our Father is through creative expression. We do not become culturally relevant when we become like the culture, but rather when we model what the culture hungers to become.

The Church is often guilty of avoiding creativity because it requires change. Resistance to change in reality is a resistance to the nature of God. The statement, *"For I the Lord do not change"* (Mal. 3:6 NASB) refers to His nature, which is perfect and unchanging. Yet He is always doing a new thing. As the winds of change blow, it will be easy to distinguish between those who are satisfied and those who are hungry. Change brings the secrets of the heart to light.

Excellence – a) The fact or state of excelling; superiority; eminence; b) An excellent quality or feature. *Synonyms*: fineness, brilliance, superiority, distinction, quality, and merit.

Excellence is the high standard set for personal achievement because of who we are in God, and who God is in us. It is not the same as perfectionism. Perfectionism is the cruel counterfeit of excellence, which flows from a religious spirit.

Excellence is impossible without passion. An excellent heart for God appears to be wasteful to those on the outside. In Matthew 26:8 we find Mary pouring ointment upon Jesus that cost a full year's income. The disciples thought it would be put to better use if it had been sold and the money given to the poor. Yet that move was so valuable to God that He said her story would be told wherever the Gospel is preached (see Matt. 26:13).

In like manner King David was extravagant when he took off his kingly garments and danced wildly before God, humbling himself before the people (see 2 Sam. 6:14-23). His wife, Michal, despised him for it. As a result she bore no children to the day of her death, either from barrenness or the lack of marital intimacy with David. Either way it's a tragic loss, as pride destroys fruitfulness, and attacks the heart of true excellence. Her biblical epitaph describes her as *Saul's daughter,* not David's wife. Her rejection of the generous heart toward God caused her to be listed with those God rejected.

David, on the other hand, was fruitful in all he put his hands to do. He was extravagant toward God. In pursuing this virtue, we are to live generously by *doing all to the glory of God, with all our might.* Such is the heart of excellence.

DISQUALIFYING OUR DISQUALIFICATION

Many feel disqualified from creativity because they have narrowly confined it to the world of art and music. They fail to realize that everyone has some measure of creativity, which should be consistently expressed throughout life.

Every 5 year old is an artist. It's an expression of their bent to create. But something happens when they enter grade school. Many educational systems narrow the definition of creativity to include only those who can draw or paint. By the time children are around 10 years of age very few of them are still considered to be artists because of that narrow definition. Today's Kingdom-oriented teachers must embrace the value of true wisdom, and develop children's creative skills outside the traditional box called "art." It is divine wisdom displayed in creativity that brings individuals to the forefront in his or her field of influence.

There are others who feel disqualified because they think that creativity always means we are to make something new or do something novel. In reality, most great ideas are actually the offspring of other concepts. Years ago I bought a jazz album on a whim. I eagerly looked forward to something fresh and new as I placed the album on the turntable. But I was horribly disappointed. It sounded like a child randomly pounding on a piano, with no melody or harmonies, no consistent rhythm, nothing to give it purpose or direction. Coincidently, I found a magazine article by the same musician a year or so later. In that magazine he described a particular season of his life in which he tried to be completely original, without being influenced by any other musician. He referred to it as a dark season of his life. It was obvious to me that I had purchased the *bad fruit* of his *bad season*. He went on to give what has become for me a profound lesson on creativity. He said that to really be creative he had to go back to what he had learned from others, and use that as a platform from which to create.

It is wisdom that can take something that is an everyday item or concept and build upon it creating something new and better. This is exactly what Solomon did. All kings of the day had cupbearers, servants, banqueting tables, and nice clothing for their servants. But there was something about his use of wisdom for everyday life that made him stand out above the rest. The queen of Sheba became speechless in response to Solomon's wisdom. It's time for the Church to display a wisdom that causes the world to become silent again.

There is a misconception that often exists in the artistic community; creativity must come from pain. There's no question but that some of the greatest works of art came from people who were troubled with life, or experienced some of the worst tragedies. The reality is this—it often takes trauma to launch a person into a place of seeing the true priorities for life. The believer doesn't need that experience. Having our old nature crucified with Christ is the only tragedy needed to launch us into our proper roles of creative influence.

THE CHURCH REVEALS

> *...that now the manifold wisdom of God might be made known by the church to the principalities and powers in the heavenly places, according to the eternal purpose which He accomplished in Christ Jesus our Lord...* (Ephesians 3:10-11).

The Church has a clear assignment: we are to exhibit the multifaceted wisdom of God, *now!* It must permeate all we are and do. This neglected element is at the heart of our call to disciple nations.

It is a part of the "witness" that turns people's heads in the same way as the nations were impacted by Solomon's wisdom. The spirit realm is watching, and more importantly, is affected by such a display. They must be reminded of their defeat, our victory, and the Father's eternal plan for the redeemed. It's our connection to wisdom that clearly manifests our eternal purpose of reigning with Christ. When we walk in wisdom, we mirror the reality of Heaven here on earth, and actually give Heaven a target for invasion. In the same way agreement with the devil empowers him to kill, steal, and destroy, so agreement with God releases God to accomplish His purposes in and through us to the world around us.[4] This is the reason He made humanity His delegated authority on this planet.[5]

A reformation has begun. And at the heart of this great move of the Spirit is the total transformation of the people of God as they discover their true identity and purpose. Great purpose elicits great sacrifice. Up until this time, many of our agendas have failed. Our attempts to make the Gospel palatable have had a serious effect on the world around us. The world has longed for a message they could *experience*. Yet many believers have simply tried to make the good news more intellectually appealing. This must stop! The natural mind *cannot* receive the things of the Spirit of God (see 1 Cor. 2:14). The wisdom of God is foolishness to men. It's time to be willing to appear foolish again, that we might provide the world with a message of power that delivers, transforms, and heals. This is true wisdom. It alone satisfies the cry of the human heart.

There are melodies that have never been heard by the human ear that would bring people to their knees in surrender to Jesus. Musicians must hear the musical sounds of Heaven and reproduce them here. I have a friend who is a wonderful worship leader. He was once taken to Heaven, where he heard them singing a song that he had written. He joyfully said, "Hey, you're singing one of my songs." But the angel replied, "No, we let you hear one of ours."

There are medical secrets that are only one prayer away from revolutionizing the way people live. Businesses strive day after day for success when the gift of wisdom can launch them into profound places of influence in a community. Politicians look to consultants on how best to run a campaign. Yet there is a wisdom in God that is so fresh and new that it will give them great favor with their constituents. There are methods of education that have been hidden in the realms of God's mysteries. He simply waits for one of His own to ask for the revelation. The list of heavenly answers is limitless. He looks for those who will ask.

THERE IS *NO* FAILURE IN FAITH

Many are discouraged because their dreams have failed. In their pain and frustration they oppose the message that a believer has the right to dream. *"Hope deferred makes the heart sick..."* but the verse doesn't stop there and neither should we: *"...but desire fulfilled is a tree of life"* (Prov. 13:12 NASB).

Here is a higher reality: when people pursue dreams but fail to see them fulfilled, they prepare the way for others who carry the same dream to eventually get the breakthrough that they were seeking. It is hard for many to take comfort in this thought, but that's because we usually think *it's all about us.* There is no failure in faith.

Often a tragic loss here on earth is viewed quite differently in Heaven. What is honored in Heaven is frequently pitied or mocked here on earth. When a person dies while trying to live out an expression of faith, people often criticize the foolishness of their decision. Few realize that their loss became the soil in which someone else could eventually realize their dream, because their loss actually paved the way to a breakthrough.

Those with failed dreams can take comfort in the fact that they prepared the way for others. It's a *John the Baptist* role. He prepared the way for the One to come. Countless times throughout history there have been those who never realized a fulfillment of their dreams. Many come to the end of their lives with the overwhelming conclusion that they failed. To our detriment, we have lived without the consciousness that a failed attempt at a dream often becomes the foundation of another person's success. Some water, others plant, and still others harvest. We all have an important role to set the stage for the King of kings to receive more glory. It's all about Him, not us.

THE NATURAL ILLUSTRATES THE SPIRITUAL

In the 1920s, a man named Mallory led an expedition to be the first to climb Mount Everest. He attempted this feat on two separate occasions, but failed. He went back to work assembling the best team of climbers available, with the finest equipment in existence. They gave extra attention to the details of their assignment, especially focusing on the issues of safety. In spite of their efforts, tragedy struck. Many in the expedition were killed in an avalanche, including Mallory. Only a few survived.

When the team returned to England, a banquet was held in their honor. The leader of the survivors stood to acknowledge the applause of those in attendance. He looked at the pictures of his comrades that were displayed around the room. Choking back the tears he spoke to the mountain on behalf of Mallory and his friends. "I speak to you, Mount Everest, in the name of all brave men living, and those yet unborn. Mount Everest, you defeated us once, you defeated us twice, you defeated us three times. But Mount Everest, we shall someday defeat you, because you can't get any bigger, but we can!" Death and disappointment could have been the end of such a quest. But instead it became the foundation for future success.

A SMALL DEVIL

There is a mountain of opposition against the purposes of God for this world. They are *principalities, powers, rulers of the darkness of this age, and spiritual hosts of wickedness in the heavenly places* (see Eph. 6:12). But the devil's dark realm is not getting any bigger.

When he rebelled against God, he was removed from his life source. He walks about as a roaring lion, hoping to intimidate through noise. His noise, the constant report of bad news, is designed to give the illusion of greatness. But it is not so.

Hell is not the realm that satan rules from. It is not a place where he takes people and torments them for eternity. It is a place of eternal torment designed for him and his demons. Those who are slaves of the devil will suffer the same demise.

On another note, demons aren't being made anymore. There's the same number wandering around the planet today as there were in Jesus' day, yet the population of people has increased into the billions, with believers numbering in the hundreds of millions. On top of that, we all know from Scripture that there are two angels for every demon. And since Jesus has *all* authority, that leaves none for the devil. The "all" that Jesus possesses has been handed over to us. His great plan is not designed so He will have to come and rescue us from the devil. It's the gates of hell that *will not* prevail against the advancing church (see Matt. 16:18). Jesus' authority has been given to us to do great exploits. With the Moravians, let's declare, "Let us win for the Lamb, the reward of His suffering!"

Our commission to pursue divine wisdom comes with mystery. That is the subject of the next chapter.

ENDNOTES

1. For more about this subject read my book *The Supernatural Power of a Transformed Mind*.

2. Even a choir is an artistic expression! See 1 Chronicles 20:21.

3. Definitions for creativity, integrity, and excellence taken from Random House Dictionary. Synonyms taken from Microsoft Word Encarta World Dictionary.

4. If God is restricted in any way, it is a self-imposed restriction.

5. For more on this subject read Chapter Two of my book *When Heaven Invades Earth*.

CHAPTER 3

The Value of Mystery

God hides things for us, not from us.

An intellectual gospel is always in danger of creating a God that looks a lot like us; one that is our size. The quest for answers sometimes leads to a rejection of mystery. As a result mystery is often treated as something intolerable, instead of a real treasure. Living with mystery is the privilege of our walk with Christ. Its importance cannot be overrated. If I understand all that is going on in my Christian life, I have an inferior Christian life. The walk of faith is to live according to the revelation we have received, in the midst of the mysteries we can't explain. That's why Christianity is called *the faith*.

All too often believers abandon or dilute their call in order to feel better about the things they cannot explain. To allow what we cannot answer to downgrade what He has shown us is to be carnal minded. Too many only obey what they understand, thus subjecting God to their judgments. God is not on trial; we are. A true *Cross-walk* is obeying where we have revelation in spite of the apparent contradiction in what we cannot explain. To obey only when we see that there will be a favorable outcome is not obedience. Obedience is supposed to be expensive. To embrace what He has shown us and to obey what He has commanded us, often in the midst of unanswerable questions, is an honor beyond measure. It is a great privilege to be a believing believer in the midst of a culture of unbelief. We must embrace this privilege. No Christian should be unmoved by the Lord's question, "When I return, will I find faith on the earth?" I have set my heart to be His pleasure by living in faith.

THE POWER OF THE OFFENDED MIND

When Jesus felt it was time to minister in His hometown of Nazareth, He went to the synagogue. As He began to teach the people, they were quite amazed at His wisdom. They were also very impressed with the healings they were seeing. But when they realized they knew Him, having watched Him grow up, they were offended in their "reasonings." "It is Jesus. We know His brothers and sisters. He grew up here! How can He do this stuff? And where did He get this wisdom?"[1] They were not offended in the typical sense; their feelings were not hurt, nor were they caught up in bitterness. They simply could not put two and two together and arrive at the conclusion—*their Jesus was a miracle worker and a man of great wisdom*. It didn't fill them with wonder and awe. Instead it caused them to become hardhearted and reject Him. This unresolved question became the mental stumbling block that was strong enough to shut down Jesus' anointing to perform miracles and teach with power. To have questions is healthy; to hold God hostage to those questions is not. It sometimes creates an atmosphere that fulfills its own prophecy about the power of God not being for today. It shuts down the very anointing that would teach them otherwise.

Not understanding is OK. Restricting our spiritual life to what we understand is not. It is immaturity at best. Such a controlling spirit is destructive to the development of a Christ-like nature. God responds to faith but will not surrender to our demands for control.

Maturity requires a heart-felt embrace of what we do not understand as an essential expression of faith.

A person's heart is more clearly seen by what they're willing to embrace without offense, than by their expression of faith only in what they already understand.

THE DEAF PRAYING FOR THE DEAF

My oldest son, Eric, is 85-90 percent deaf in both ears. He has an amazing gift for life. He functions beautifully in the "hearing world" and has never had to learn sign language. His adjustments to life are miraculous, while his self-esteem is unaffected by this handicap. He is strong and Christ-centered. He is our Missions Pastor.

I was fasting and praying for his healing some years ago, and God spoke to me very clearly that He was going to heal him. It *has* happened in the atonement, and will be seen in my lifetime. We don't treat it as a *someday off in the future God will heal Him* kind of thing. We view it as a *right now* word. Yet he still can't hear without the assistance of a hearing aid.

It's interesting that the healing of deafness is one of the most common miracles I see in my meetings and in our church. Even more interesting to note is that in the last couple of months Eric has laid hands on two people who were deaf and God opened their ears. How could that happen without him being healed first? I don't know. But I do know that mental offense, stumbling over this apparent contradiction in our minds, will shut down this anointing. That is something we are not willing to do. Eric and I will continue to live in the understanding we have, and embrace the mystery we are required to live with, knowing that God is perfectly faithful and good beyond measure, all the time. He is worthy of our trust.

HOW WE LEARN

I'll never forget when God first began to open up the Scriptures to me. As I read, my heart leapt within me over the richness of what

I was reading. Yet I couldn't have taught on that particular passage if my life depended on it. My spirit was doing the learning and my mind would have to wait. The mind is trained through the experience of divine encounters and supernatural experiences initiated through the revelations from Scriptures. Revelation that doesn't lead to a divine encounter will only make us more religious, teaching us to embrace external standards without the internal realities.

God is not opposed to the mind; He created the mind to be a complement to all that He had made. He is opposed to the unrenewed mind. It is at war with God, being incapable of obeying Him (see Rom. 8:7). The believer who governs his Christian life through the mind is the carnal Christian that the apostle Paul warned about (see 1 Cor. 2–3). The soul can only lead us into religion[2]– form without power. It is what makes way for Ishmaels instead of Isaacs.[3]

It's important to understand the learning process. Our spirit is where the Holy Spirit dwells. Our spirit is alive and well and is ready to receive great things from God. When I filter everything through my mind and remove what isn't immediately logical, I extract much of what I really need. Only what goes beyond my understanding is positioned to renew my mind (see Phil. 4:7). If we can learn more about the actual voice and presence of the Lord, we will stop being so paranoid about being deceived by the things we can't explain. Usually those who use the natural mind to protect themselves from deception are the most deceived. They've relied on their own finite logic and reason to keep them safe, which is in itself a deception. They usually have an explanation for all that's going on in their walk with the Lord, but criticize those who long for more.

Our hearts can embrace things that our heads can't. Our hearts will lead us where our logic would never dare to go. No one ever attributes the traits of courage and valor to the intellect or the strength of human reasoning. Courage rises up from within and gives influence over the mind. In the same way, true faith affects the mind. Faith does not come from our understanding. It comes from the heart. We do not believe because we understand; we understand because we believe (see Heb. 11:6). We'll know when our mind is truly renewed, because the impossible will look logical.

MYSTERY—A CROSS FOR THE MIND

What we don't understand is sometimes as important as what we do. It's one thing to obey when He has given us understanding about a matter, and quite another to obey while facing questions and circumstances that seem to contradict what we understand. So many fail at this point, and then bring the Bible down to their level of experience. Many do this to feel better about the fact that they are living in compromise—a compromise of their revelation from Scripture. Our challenge is instead to bring our lifestyle up to the standard of God's Word.

To embrace revelation[4] with one hand, and embrace mystery with the other, forms a perfect cross. This is a cross that everyone who is hungry to do the works of Jesus will have to carry. God must violate our logic to invite us away from the deception of relying on our own reasoning.

GOD HIDES THINGS TO BE FOUND

When my children were small we hid Easter eggs for them to find. The measure of difficulty in the search was always determined by the age and capabilities of the child. We never went outside, dug a 3-foot deep hole and buried a chocolate egg hoping a 2 year old would find it. When my children were that young, we'd put the egg on a table, or on a chair. And as they got older we would make it more difficult, but never impossible. Parents delight in their child's curiosity, and love to see them enjoy the process of discovery. Children enjoy the pleasure of the search, and revel in the affirmation of their parent's delight in their searching and discovery. "...*Seek and you shall find...*" (Matt. 7:7). This curiosity and delight in discovery are meant to be a part of what it is to "*seek first the kingdom*"

(Matt. 6:33) as well as to *"receive the kingdom of God as a little child"* (Luke 18:17).

> *It is the glory of God to conceal a matter, but the glory of kings is to search out a matter* (Proverbs 25:2).

People wonder why God doesn't always speak in more open terms—audibly, with visible signs, and other such ways. I don't know how or why it works this way, but the Bible indicates that *God receives more glory when He conceals*, rather than making things obvious. It is more glorious for Him to hide, and have us seek. In the introduction to the parable of the seed and the sower we find that Jesus did not merely use parables as illustrations, but at times to conceal truth so that only the hungry would understand (see Matt. 13:11,18-23). It is the mercy of God to withhold revelation from those who have no hunger for truth, because if they don't hunger for it, the chances are they won't obey it when they hear it. Revelation always brings responsibility, and hunger is the thing that prepares our hearts to carry the weight of that responsibility. By keeping revelation from those without hunger, God actually protects them from certain failure to carry the responsibility it would lay on them. And so He conceals. Yet, He doesn't conceal from us; He conceals *for* us!

But there's another part to this equation—*"it's the glory of kings to search out a matter"*! We are kings and priests to our God (see Rev. 1:6). Our royal identity never shines brighter than when we pursue hidden things with the confidence that we have legal access to such things. Mysteries are our inheritance. Our kingship, our role in ruling and reigning with Christ,[5] comes to the forefront when we seek Him for answers to the dilemmas of the world around us.

Jesus answered them, *"To you it has been granted to know the mysteries of the kingdom of heaven, but to them it has not been granted"* (Matt. 13:11 NASB). We, as believers, have legal access to the realm of God's mysteries. It's that simple. The hidden things are placed in waiting for the believer to discover. They are ours by inheritance.

TRUTH HELD IN TENSION

It is very hard to imagine the Church bringing answers to the issues of life when much of our eschatology anticipates world conditions getting worse and worse. When we also believe that the darkness of world circumstances is the signal for Christ's return, we have a conflict that ultimately costs us a practical vision—to invade and transform the world system. It's not my intention to declare when or how Jesus is returning for His Church. My only point is that wrong assumptions about the unobvious can harden us to the obvious.[6] If we assume we know what certain types and shadows used in the prophets mean it can incorrectly influence our understanding of the clear commandments of the Lord. Wrongly interpreting when and how He is returning can undermine our approach to the Great Commission.

Jesus is returning for a spotless Bride, whose Body is in equal proportion to her Head. The Father alone knows when that moment will be. We don't. Our job is to do everything possible to bring about, "*Thy kingdom come, Thy will be done, on earth as it is in Heaven.*" If my faith for His return has its anchor in the darkness of the world around me, then I will do little to change it. We will try to get converts, of course, but to bring answers to the issues of this planet will not be a priority. Yet this is the practical tool that turns the hearts of the kings of our day (see Prov. 22:29).

Our commission is clear: we are to disciple nations! And to insure that this seemingly impossible task would be possible, He caused the One called *the desire of the nations* to live within us. This revelation of Him is ultimately a revelation about us, for we are His Body. Being made in His image gives us the privilege and responsibility to reflect His greatness to the world around us. The nations are looking for a people who can bring the answers to the issues facing our world.

HANNAH'S MYSTERY

Hannah's womb was closed. She was barren and without hope of bearing children apart from a miracle. As cruel as it may sound to the natural man, God used this to bring her into her greatest success. In her barrenness she developed a desperate heart. The purpose of a promise is not to inspire us to strategize and make plans, but instead it works to make us desperate for God to show up. This means that barrenness in any area is our invitation to excel. Hannah became a co-laborer in fulfilling her own destiny. Solomon states, "*An inheritance gained hurriedly at the beginning will not be blessed in the end*" (Prov. 20:21 NASB). Not everything comes to us easily, nor should it. The God who hides things for us also gives us His Kingdom as our inheritance. Israel was given the Promised Land, but was told it would come to them little by little so that the beasts wouldn't become too numerous for them. His promises cover everything—His promises are yes and *amen*! (See 2 Cor. 1:20.) All is covered by the redemptive work on the Cross, but it is gained little by little, sometimes through our co-laboring effort.

This became a great personal lesson in my quest for miracles. Mario Murillo has had more to do in stirring up the passions of a revivalist in my life than any other person. Almost 20 years ago I asked him about the life of miracles, telling him of my frustration in having theory without fruit. I had never witnessed anyone getting healed, even though I tried many times. He encouraged me with one of the most powerful prophetic words of my life. In it the Lord spoke of His intent to make miracles a regular part of my life. I have prayed over that promise for many years. In recent years I have seen thousands of people healed.

Mario, and his wife, Mechelle, recently came to our home for lunch. I showed him the prophetic word he spoke over me in 1988. I did so to express my thanks to him for being such an encouragement to me. He brought up the story of Hannah and her closed womb. He said that God has closed up the realm of the miraculous to me, not as punishment, but to draw me into the desperation needed to maintain it as a lifestyle once I received my breakthrough.

It was a long and painful lesson. But I got it. And I think I really understand.

MARY'S MYSTERY

Mary, the mother of Jesus, lived with mystery in a most notable fashion. She carried revival better than anyone, since Jesus is revival personified. Mary was given the ultimate mystery—both in word and experience.

Mary gave birth to the Christ-child as declared by the angel Gabriel. The things spoken of by those who recognized Jesus' purpose and divinity were pondered in her heart. The word *things* in this story is the word "rhema" in the original language, which is the *freshly spoken word of God.* She pondered the things *spoken to her by God,* even though she didn't understand them. Her pondering gave place for the roots to be established and the word to grow until the promise became manifest. God's Word grows in the heart of the yielded believer.

Her encounter with mystery could be summarized as follows:

1. As a young girl Mary had an angelic encounter with Gabriel.
2. Gabriel gave Mary a word that was incomprehensible; she was to give birth to the Messiah while she remained a virgin—a biblically unprecedented experience.
3. She yielded to what was beyond understanding by saying, *"Be it unto me, according to Thy word."*
4. Mary nearly lost Joseph, her fiancé, to the news that "God made me pregnant." An angel appeared to Joseph to convince him it was true, thus saving their marriage.
5. She began to "manifest" under the influence of the ultimate revival—Jesus. (You can only hide the reality of pregnancy/revival so long.)
6. Those who knew that her son was the Messiah would often speak to her of His greatness. She pondered the things they

said in her heart, thus becoming pregnant again—this time with promise.

In essence, the glorious story of Mary is repeated every time we are impregnated with God's Word of promise. Christ is still being formed in His people. This spiritual reality is not to be thought inferior to the natural reality that Mary experienced. In no way do I mean to dishonor Mary. She will be considered "highly favored of the Lord" forever! Rather, I want to increase respect for the work of the Spirit of God in every heart.

THE KINGDOM NOW, BUT NOT YET

When I first heard this phrase, *the Kingdom now but not yet*, over 20 years ago, it was used as a statement of promise. It was helpful for me to realize that we have access to things right now that I had always thought were inaccessible. The phrase helped to bring into focus the reality that some things will be enjoyed in time, and some things only in eternity. But that same phrase has also been used to define limitations and restrictions, and not instill hope. It is used to ease people's dissatisfaction with unrealized promises now. But I have a problem with this approach. It makes people satisfied with less than is available now. I rarely hear it used to describe our potential or promise; it carries with it boundaries and barriers that Jesus did not teach or make.

It is true that a full manifestation of the Kingdom of God is more than our physical bodies can endure. But it is also true that when we are in Heaven we will still be able to say, *now, but not yet*, about the Kingdom, because there is no end to the increase of His government. Throughout eternity the Kingdom will be expanding, and we will always be advancing. I teach our people that if *now, but not yet* is used to define promise and potential, accept it. If it is spoken to build awareness of our limitations and restrictions, reject it. We don't need more people without authentic Kingdom experiences telling us what we can and cannot have in our lifetime. Those who walk out their faith with an experiential paradigm understand that we will always live in the tension of what we have seen and what we have yet to see, and that we are always moving on to *more* in God. This is an *understanding by experience* issue.

Someone has to go beyond the boundaries of historical accomplishments and attempt something that has been considered impossible by their contemporaries. The Church is often known as the group that *changes not*. Very little of what exists today would exist at all if those who preceded us did not seek to surpass the boundaries experienced by their predecessors. And so it is with the Church. It is this adventure that God has called us to. And it is this adventure that we call *the normal Christian life*.

THE LANGUAGE OF MYSTERY

As God draws us into a place of embracing the realm of His mysteries, He establishes the life of faith in us. Yet He longs to unlock the mysteries for those desiring to make a difference in the world around them. Hidden things are revealed to those who hunger for Him, and can recognize His voice. That is the subject of the next chapter.

ENDNOTES

1. My paraphrase.

2. The most common definition of the soul is the *mind, will,* and *emotions.*

3. Ishmael was the son of Abraham's efforts, while Isaac was the son of God's promise.

4. More on this in the chapter called, "The Spirit of Revelation."

5. It is important to note, *ruling* from God's perspective means to be the servant of all. Too many have embraced this theology, and have used it as an excuse to pursue ruling over others in the way Jesus warned against. Our strong suit has been, and always will be, serving.

6. One of the greatest errors in end-time theology comes from working to interpret types and symbols (the unobvious) until they redefine the clear commands of the Lord (the obvious). For example, many know much more about God and Magog, the ten nation confederacy, the seven years of tribulation, the anti-Christ, etc. than they do about the simple command to pray *"on earth as it is in Heaven."*

CHAPTER 4

The Language of the Spirit

"God hides things for you, not from you."

A yielded imagination becomes a sanctified imagination; and it's the sanctified imagination that is positioned for visions and dreams. There is great paranoia over the use of the imagination in the Church of the Western world.[1] As a result; unbelievers often lead the way in creative expression—through the arts and inventions. They have no bias against imagination. The imagination is like a canvas to a painter. If it's clean, the artist has much to work with. God would love to use our imagination to paint His impressions upon; He just looks for those who are yielded. However, those who are preoccupied with "not being worthy" are too self-centered to be trusted with much revelation. At some point it has to stop being about us long enough to utilize the benefits of being in Christ for the sake of those around us. Such a position gives us unlimited access to the mysteries of God that enable us to touch the needs of a dying world.

Jesus is the Word of God. It's hard for Him to not have something to say. Occasionally, we go through times when we feel God is not speaking to us. While that may be so, most of the time He has simply changed His language, and He expects us to adjust with Him.

Missing the Audible Voice of God

"Father, glorify Your name." Then a voice came from heaven saying "I have both glorified it, and will glorify it again." Therefore the people who stood by and heard it said that it had thundered. Others said, "An angel has spoken to Him" (John 12:28-29).

The audible voice of the Father came from Heaven while Jesus was speaking to a crowd. The people acknowledged hearing something, but none of them knew what it was. Not only did they fail to realize it was the voice of God, it never occurred to them that this unusual event had any meaning for their lives. Jesus responded to their unbelief by saying, *"This voice did not come because of Me, but for your sake"* (see John 12:27-30). In His mercy God spoke to provide a way out of the lifestyle of unbelief for every bystander. But their hardness of heart blocked their perception of what was said, who was speaking, and made what they heard unintelligible. We know that God spoke clearly (see 1 Cor. 14:9). Yet the people did not *understand* because of their predisposition toward unbelief (see John 12:37). Some thought it was thunder—an impersonal act of nature. Others thought it might have been an angel—spiritual, but just not for them.[2] It is a true statement that it's the hungry heart that hears best.

Unbelief Masquerades as Wisdom

The story of John 12 addresses one of my greatest concerns for the church in the Western world—the prevalence of unbelief. It has masqueraded long enough as wisdom and must be exposed for being the great sin that it is. Unbelief has the outward appearance of a conservative approach to life, but works to subject God Himself to the mind and control of people. It feeds off the opinion of others, all the while stroking itself for not falling into the extremes that others have stumbled into. What is seldom realized by those who live in such a religious trap is that an unbelieving mind-set is completely unable to represent Jesus in His power and glory.

It is troubling to me that so many Christians need me to prove that God actually does what I say I've seen Him do—as though the Scriptures were not enough proof. What is even more astonishing is that when the miracles happen before their eyes, they still want doctors' reports, x-rays, etc. before they will give God any praise. It is grievous to see an empty wheelchair with someone walking, a formerly depressed person rejoicing, or one who could not hear now hearing and giving praise, but the bystander still wants proof those were really miracles. I realize that charlatans exist. But the massive effort to protect ourselves from being fooled is more a sign of unbelief than it is of our wisdom keeping us from deception. Such a fear only exists where unbelief has reigned for a long time.

However, *"Love believes all things"* (1 Cor. 13:7 NASB). A deeper encounter with the love of God frees a person from the tendency to protect themselves out of fear through unreasonable caution. And considering that *"faith works through love"* (Gal. 5:6), it is reasonable to say that even the faith to believe God for miracles can come by experiencing His love. Overwhelming encounters with the extravagant love of our heavenly Father will do much to dismantle unbelief.

It is not wisdom that continually asks God to demonstrate Himself for us so that we might believe. While there is no question that exposure to the miraculous can help us grow in faith, such a demand is not a hunger for Him but is instead an effort to put God on trial. He is not on trial. We are. The un-renewed mind is at war with God and puts demands on Him to perform for us. That unhealthy attitude puts us in the role of a judge. Such arrogance is the father of unbelief. Jesus confronted these attitudes in his many encounters with the religious crowd.

THE ULTIMATE MEAL

The heart of abiding faith "leans into God," anticipating His voice, looking for His next move. Like Jesus, we are to be able to say, *"My food is to do the will of Him who sent me"* (John 4:34 NASB). I am strengthened in hearing God speak. I am nourished through my own obedience to His voice. The situations of life take on meaning and purpose because of the abiding faith to follow Jesus. Hearing from God is the essential element of the Christian life, for *"man shall not live by bread alone, but by every word that proceeds from the mouth of God"* (Matt. 4:4). His voice is our life.

There are many tables to eat at in life. There is the table of *public opinion.* The food is sweet, but it sours in the stomach. There is the table of *personal achievement.* That's a power meal for sure, yet the crash is as rapid as the ascent. There's only one table with rich food that settles well and brings supernatural strength; it's the table of God's will.

MY PERSONAL STORY IN REVIVAL

When I became the pastor of Bethel Church, in Redding, California, I came because of a cry for revival by the leadership of the church. I was the pastor of Mountain Chapel, in Weaverville, California, where we were experiencing a wonderful outpouring of the Holy Spirit. Bethel was the mother church of our church in Weaverville, where my family and I had been for 17 years. The invitation came for me to return and be Bethel's Senior Pastor. When I spoke to the new congregation about my coming, I told them that I was born for revival; if they didn't want the move of the Spirit of God, along with the messes that come from such an outpouring (see Prov. 14:4), they didn't want me, because this was not negotiable! They responded positively with close to unanimous support.

The outpouring began almost immediately. Lives were changed, bodies were healed, divine encounters increased in amazing proportions—and approximately 1,000 people left the church.

What was happening was outside their point of reference and off the map of their own experience.

Few things are more devastating to pastors than when people leave the church. It feels like personal rejection (and often times it really is). Those in ministry are certainly not immune to these feelings. Pastors are a unique breed—there are times when people who hate us leave the church and we still feel bad. Yet during this strange season of *exodus*, my wife and I were immune to the devastation, which is only possible if God has actually given a supernatural grace to joyfully live *opposite* of your circumstances. (The counterfeit that many fall for is to be callous of heart to the point that no one can affect you, good or bad. And still others choose to live in denial about the impact that such a loss is causing in their hearts. Neither is healthy or acceptable.) Because of the grace given to us, not one day was spent in discouragement or questioning God. Our food really was doing His will, which provides all the nourishment and strength we need.

It was the generosity of God that made this possible. Along with the increased manifestation of His presence, He made His will too obvious to ever miss. God often spoke to us in a dream, a vision, or a clear impression in our minds. Sometimes He brought forth a prophetic word that confirmed or added understanding to a direction we were to take. There was never a question. The fruit of the increased measure of His presence, along with the bounty of transformed lives, was all we needed to smile in the face of such apparent loss. To this day, we've considered it a privilege to gain that kind of increase through such a loss.

Today we are growing fast. The miracles are increasing in astonishing ways. Yet I secretly savor the moments of the initial outpouring when it was illogical to the natural mind to be so happy when so many things appeared to be so wrong. The opposition was fierce at times. The slander and rumors increased daily with a vengeance. For close to a year our denominational office received complaints and accusations about us every single day. Yet only God can make such a season so wonderful, because only His will is so completely nourishing. It has been, and continues to be, my favorite meal.

The beauty of His will is lost for the person who does not know the language of the Spirit. It is vital to learn how God speaks. His first language is not English. In fact, it would be safe to say it's not Hebrew either. While He uses the languages of men to communicate with us, He is more inclined to speak through a myriad of other methods. In the remainder of this chapter I will attempt to address some of the "languages of the Spirit." There are many great materials written on this subject, so I will only emphasize the areas that are a bit more obscure, such as the section called "Dark Sayings." This is far from a complete list. It represents the limited discoveries of my own adventure with God.

THE LANGUAGE OF THE SCRIPTURES

The Scriptures are the basis for all "hearing" from God. While God will not violate His Word, He often violates our understanding of His Word. Remember, God is bigger than His book. The Bible does not contain God; it *reveals* Him.

This truth can be represented by two Greek words for *word*, "logos" and "rhema."

Logos is often used to speak of the written Word, our Holy Bible. Bible reading is the most common way of receiving instruction and learning to recognize His voice. Page after page is filled with practical instructions for life. Learning the principles of God's Word helps us to learn to recognize His voice by establishing truth in our hearts. The Psalmist affirmed that purpose, saying, *"Your word I have treasured in my heart, that I may not sin against You"* (Ps. 119:11 NASB). This is where we find the Kingdom principles for life. They work for anyone who applies them.

Rhema is the freshly spoken word. It is always an expression of that which is *being uttered*. Therefore it carries an aspect of immediacy with it. Often times God breathes upon His Word and gives life to something written for "now." The spoken word is never to replace the written Word. The more of the written Word we have in our hearts, the greater capacity we have to hear the spoken word, because He speaks to that which has been deposited in our hearts and calls it forth.

THE LANGUAGE OF THE AUDIBLE VOICE

The voice of the Lord is not an impression that we have to find language for. It is a direct word-for-word communication from God to us. The audible voice may come to the natural ear while we're awake or while we're asleep. It can also come to our spiritual ears. (The reason I make this distinction is that after it has happened, you can't always remember if it was out loud or internal. It is far more than an impression. It is as clear as hearing someone speak.)

On at least two occasions I have been awakened with the audible voice of the Lord. But in reflection I never thought that my wife would have heard it. She didn't. That's why I say it can come to the natural ear, as it did in John 12, or in our spirit. He once woke me with His voice, saying, "He watches over the watch of those who watch the Lord." That phrase then ran through my mind the rest of the night. It became apparent that He wanted my full attention so I could learn to watch Him only. In doing so He would watch over all that concerned me.

THE LANGUAGE OF THE STILL SMALL VOICE

This is the quiet voice or impression of the heart. This is probably the most common way that people hear from God. It is sometimes thought to be our own "inner voice" in that it is our own thoughts and ideas. While we do have such a voice, it is wisdom to learn to recognize *His* still small voice. It is quiet. So we must become quiet to recognize it consistently. Someone gave me a helpful clue to discerning His voice; they said, "You know you've heard from God whenever you have an idea that's better than one you could think up yourself."

THE LANGUAGE OF VISIONS

Visions come both to the natural eye and to the eyes of the heart. The second are the pictures in the mind, which are the visual equivalent of the still small voice—they are as easy to miss as they are to get. *Leaning into God*[3] is what makes this one come into focus.

External—Many people refer to this as an "open vision." Though I have never had one, I have many friends who have, including my senior associate, Kris Vallotton. One such method that God has used with him is when something like a movie screen appears over a person's head, and God plays back portions of that person's life. Describing it to them tends to get their attention, preparing the way for them to receive significant personal ministry.

Internal—On a ministry trip to Germany, preceding the evening healing meeting, I was praying with the leadership of a remarkable ministry. I had a "snapshot" picture flash in my mind. In it I saw someone seated to my right, and then saw only their spine, as in an x-ray. I somehow knew it was arthritic. In this vision I pointed to them and said, "The Lord Jesus heals you!" This vision sounds much more dramatic than it really was. It was a brief snapshot that I gave attention to. It was one that I could have easily missed. When it was my time to speak, I started by asking if there was anyone there with arthritis in the spine. A woman to my right raised her hand. After asking her to stand I declared, "The Lord Jesus heals you!" She began to tremble. When I asked her "where is your pain?" she responded with intense weeping, saying, "It's impossible! It's impossible! It's gone!" She was healed through a declaration that was brought about by an internal vision.

At another time, during a tent meeting with Todd Bentley in Roseville, California, I had a unique experience involving another internal vision. During the worship I saw the vertebrae of a neck and realized it was injured. But I also saw the number 94 float by. It was not dramatic, but very subtle—easy to miss. When I got up to speak, I asked for those to come forward who had injured their neck in 1994 in some sort of accident. To my surprise 12 people came to the front for prayer. I was able to speak to eight or nine of them following the time of prayer and each one had been healed.

THE LANGUAGE OF DREAMS

Obviously, dreams mostly happen at night. But there is a form of dreaming that is similar to a *daydream*. They happen when you're awake and are more likely to be ignored because you think it's *your imagination*. In their more intense form they are more like a trance. Once again, leaning into God brings this tool into a clearer perspective, giving us the needed discernment to recognize what is from God and what is actually our imagination.

Daydream. While sitting in a conference, I began to daydream about a prayer house. I could see four walls of windows to the north, south, east, and west. Over each window was the phrase from Isaiah, "*Say to the North, 'Give them back!'*" The same appeared over each of the windows facing their respective directions. In the carpet was the compass star, again pointing to the north, south, east, and west. In the center of the room was a fountain that flowed continuously. I knew it was to be called the Alabaster House. (An alabaster vial is what was used to contain the priceless—actually worth about a year's salary—ointment that the woman poured over Jesus before His death as the ultimate expression of worship (see Mark 14:3). The disciples became angry because this woman *wasted* her perfume with such a senseless act, when it could have been sold and the money given to the poor. Jesus had a different perspective; He called it worship.) I felt we were to build a place where people could *waste themselves on Jesus!* When I shared this experience with our church board, one of the members[4] asked to meet with me the next day. He was a contractor who brought in plans he had drawn two years earlier of the very prayer house I had described. Needless to say, we built the Alabaster House, even though its construction was during the time when about 1,000 people were leaving the church. We built it with cash—another testimony of God's wonderful mercy and grace.

Night Dream. As I was preparing to come to Bethel Church to be their new pastor, I had a dream warning me of the potential danger in the coming transition. In the dream I was taking an exit off of a freeway. I was then to cross over the roadway on an overpass, and get back on the freeway going in the opposite direction. When doing so I noticed that the road was icy and that I would need to be cautious as to how fast I made the turn or I would roll my vehicle off the embankment back onto the freeway. I woke up realizing that God just warned me not to make the needed changes too quickly. While some might have felt our transition happened rather fast, it was much slower than it would have been without that dream. Each step was preceded by a clear Word from God.

He let me know when that season of "cautious turning" was over through another dream. In it I saw the same freeway, but this time I was going the opposite direction. There was bright green grass on both sides of the road, and the pavement was wet from the melted ice. As strange as it may sound, the water didn't pose any danger to traveling at high speeds but instead was a sign of His fresh outpouring. The ice, that made a quick transition dangerous and unwise, had melted. There were no other cars to slow down or impede our progress. In giving me this dream He spoke, saying, "It's time to pull out the stops." This second dream occurred around 18 months after the first one. The majority of the people had left that were going to leave and I was now given liberty to go at a pace more suitable to the increasing winds of change.

THE LANGUAGE OF DARK SAYINGS (PROV. 1:6 KJV)

God sometimes speaks to us by hiding truths in phrases, stories, riddles, and circumstances. The meaning is there for us to find. When we *lean into God*, anticipating His voice, it becomes easier to discern when those circumstances are from God, or are merely unusual events in life. This unique language from God is an invitation to enter His great adventure.

Parables. At my request, a member of our maintenance team took a dear prophet friend and me around our church's near 70 acres to find the corners of the property line. We drove stakes into the ground at the corners. Each stake had a different colored flag attached, representing a particular gift and calling upon our church. This was not something I had done before and found it to be a unique experience to walk the grounds and pray according to what the prophet sees. While it was different for me, I trusted him.

Upon driving the last stake into the ground, four geese flew by. The prophet told me the goose is the *watchdog* of the old world, and they represented the angels who stood at the four corners of the property guarding what God is doing there.

Jesus was teaching through the use of parables when He gave the disciples the promise that the Father has given us access to His mysteries (see Matt. 13:11). There are patterns of interpretation that can help us to find His intended message. For example, the number four represents the earth—the four corners of the earth; north, south, east, and west; etc. Understanding these things can help us to more clearly hear everything from simple words of affirmation to great words of revelation.

Riddles. I include this story in the *riddle* category because it needs an interpretation. Sometimes the Lord speaks in ways that can be researched through biblical principles of interpretation. For example, the number 50 means Jubilee. It comes from the Jubilee principle (forgiving all debt and releasing all slaves) that Israel was instructed to follow every 50 years. The following story could not be interpreted in that way. God alone could explain.

In October 2003 I woke up at 5:55 A.M. after running into those numbers several times in just a few days. While lying in bed I said out loud, "What are you trying to tell me?" Immediately I was asleep as though someone knocked me out. He then spoke audibly saying, "The anointing for the day of the cancellation of debt is upon you." I instantly woke up realizing that I had been asleep for maybe three minutes. Since that day, all debt is gone from our lives, with the exception of our mortgage, which we believe is next. The numbers were like a puzzle that needed explanation from the manufacturer.

There are great books that give us principles of interpretation for numbers and symbols in the Bible and in life. However, I doubt that any of them would say that 555 means the cancellation of debt. I recommend people use those books as guides, but seek the Lord to see if there is something else He wants to say. Parables tend to be more symbolic, while riddles need divine explanation.

Unusual Coincidences. I have paid little attention to these for most of my life. It's only been in the last couple of years that His language has become more obvious to me in this way. While it would be wrong to say that every coincidence has the voice of God in it, God is speaking through them more often than you might think.

He got my attention recently with the following chain of events. I checked into my hotel preparing for some meetings in the great state of Texas. The man behind the counter gave me room key #308. I gave it no thought. When I went to the next city I noticed I was again given a key for room #308. It seemed like a strange coincidence, but I can't say I felt it was anything but an unusual coincidence. Then I woke up at 3:08 in the morning. God finally had my attention. I asked, "What are you trying to tell me?" The answer didn't come for several days; while sitting at my desk in my office it hit me, about 18 years earlier I had been seeking the Lord whether or not I should attempt to write.

It had been in my heart for quite some time, but I was never a great student, and had missed much of what I would need to know in order to be a writer. But I had this desire that wouldn't go away. In response to my question about writing, He woke me in the middle of the night and said these words, "Isaiah 30, verse 8." When I opened the Bible to see what it said I read, "*Now go, and write.*" Very soon afterward, I began to write small articles for our church bulletin. I made time for it in my regular schedule so that I could learn more of what I needed to know through experience.

Now 18 years later I had written a fair amount, but I had filled my most recent schedule with conferences and other traveling engagements. At the time of the "308" word, it had been months since I had set any time aside for writing. In fact, my schedule was making that goal more and more impossible. The number 308 was a reminder of my question to God, His answer, and the subsequent call on my life. The conviction of the Lord came upon me and I repented. I met with my staff to go over my calendar for the next several months and set aside blocks of time for writing. Even the writing of this book is in response to that word.

During that same trip to Texas I had another experience that was new to me. I had a word of knowledge in a meeting about someone with a broken tailbone. A woman yelled out that it was her and that she broke it giving birth to her child. She was instantly healed without prayer. Moments later I had a word of knowledge about someone with broken ribs. The same woman spoke loudly from the back of the room, "I broke my ribs carrying my child (in pregnancy)." She was again healed instantly. In the next town someone came to me to testify that they had just been healed of an injury they suffered while giving birth to their child. (I don't remember ever having someone healed of something of this nature—now, two cities in a row women were healed of birth-related issues. That is the language of the Spirit—unusual coincidences.) I stopped the meeting and asked for all those who had ongoing physical problems caused either by pregnancy or giving birth to stand up. Around ten women stood. Over the next few minutes at least eight of them testified that they were healed.

Unusual Circumstances. The burning bush of Moses' experience would fall into this category. These are highly unusual situations that usually seem to have no meaning in and of themselves. God brings those events into our lives to get our attention, hoping we will "turn aside" from our agendas and plans. *"When the Lord saw that he turned aside to look, God called to him from the midst of the bush and said, 'Moses, Moses!'"* (Exod. 3:4 NASB). When Moses turned aside, God spoke.

We have a pre-service prayer meeting on Friday nights. Many meet in the church dining room to pray for the meeting. One night I got there a bit early to pray alone. Soon after my arrival, a roadrunner with a lizard in its mouth, came up to the wall of windows facing the west. He started to dance and jump at the window as though he were trying to get inside. I live in Redding, California, and have spent quite a bit of time outdoors. I had never seen a roadrunner in my life and never even heard of one in northern California. I got within 3 feet of him and thought, "This is too strange to not be prophetic." Minutes later he left. The time came for others to come to pray, and the room began to fill up. Then the roadrunner returned. One of my staff members said, "Oh, the roadrunner's back." I asked him what he meant. He said, "Yeah. He was here last week." I responded, "You're kidding!" He obviously wasn't.

For the next several months the roadrunner came to most every prayer meeting, usually with a lizard in its mouth. Some of our youth leaders began to meet in the dining room to pray before their main meeting on Wednesday nights. The roadrunner started to come to that prayer meeting as well, usually with a lizard in its mouth. I used to have a Signs and Wonders class on Sunday morning. One morning I talked about the *signs that make you wonder*, and used the roadrunner as an illustration. Almost on cue he came up to the window as before. The people pointed and said, "You mean him!" I was shocked. He came almost "on cue."

News began to spread about this strange recurring event. Many tried to help by doing research to find the meaning. I was told that in the natural the roadrunner is related to the eagle. They're one of the few animals that will kill and eat a rattlesnake, which we do have in our area. (I was happy about that.) I already knew that eagles represent the prophetic and snakes usually speak of the devil. Knowing that the enemy would be trampled down through the increase of the prophetic brought great joy.

During this time we starting building our 24-hour prayer chapel called The Alabaster House. The roadrunner started to shift his focus from our prayer meetings to that building. He would actually perch himself on a rock which many of our folks had taken to calling the Eagle Rock, because of its unusual resemblance to the head of an eagle. It was as though the roadrunner, who loved prayer meetings, was overseeing the prayer house building project.

One day he got inside the church facility, right above the original prayer room. One of our custodians, Jason (an extremely prophetic student in our school of ministry), found the bird in a large second story meeting room. Jason turned on some worship music and sat in the middle of the room on the floor and worshiped the Lord. The roadrunner came over right in front of him and seemed to join him. He would occasionally leave Jason and go to the window as though he wanted outside, but then he came back and stood right in front of Jason as he worshiped.

Jason started to feel bad for taking so much time for worship while he was supposed to be cleaning that he turned the music off and went downstairs to clean other rooms. The roadrunner went with him. Suddenly someone opened the door in the long hallway and startled the bird. He flew to the end of the hall, hit our plate glass window, and died instantly.

This bird had become like a beloved mascot to us, reminding us of the importance of prayer. He loved prayer meetings and had become a prophetic symbol of God's promised increase for us as a church family. He came during a time when many members had already left or were leaving, and the finances were extremely tight. The lizard in his mouth spoke to us of God bringing all that was needed for this move of God. As eagles represent the prophets, it was obvious that the prophetic was actually getting stronger and stronger within our church body.

Jason found me to tell me this horrible news. I asked him to show me where he had put the bird so we could go and raise it from the dead. With a sense of purpose and confidence we walked around back where the roadrunner was laying. It made perfect sense to me that God would want the roadrunner alive. Why should He want our living prophetic message dead? Strangely, I actually felt the anointing lift when I got around 5 to 6 feet away from the bird. It was puzzling to me. God's presence was upon me in a strong way until I got close. It was like He was saying my resolve was good, but my application and timing was not. The roadrunner was not raised from the dead. We were quite sad. Then the Lord spoke, "What I am bringing into the house has to have a way of being released from the house, or it will die in the house."

That word applied to the money we desperately needed, the manifest gifts of the Spirit we were crying out for, the specific anointings we were growing in, and the people who were being saved. The word was costly and clear; *we only get to keep what we give away.*

Prophecy. This is one of the most important areas of my life. God has been very faithful to put prophetic people in my life at just the right times—people of great integrity. As a result, we have a strong prophetic culture. To encourage risk on the part of prophetic people we emphasize the responsibility of the hearer to discern whether or not a word is from God. In the Old Testament the Spirit of God was upon the prophet alone, so he bore all the responsibility. Today the Spirit of the Lord is within every believer, so the responsibility is now given to the people of God to discern whether or not a specific word is from God. When it is from God, we respond according to the direction given in the Word. When it's not from God, we try to learn from it and sharpen our prophetic skills.[5]

Prophecy comes to us from another person. While this can be a very dangerous form of hearing from God, it can also be one of the most dramatic and faith-building. Once it has been confirmed as having it's origins from God, we must act accordingly.

Kris Vallotton prophesied over me early one Sunday morning saying that God was going to support me publicly by bringing in the total amount of money needed to build our prayer house in one offering. This was the very day we felt we were to present the project and follow the presentation by receiving an offering. In the natural this was the worst time to expect a large offering as this was toward the end of the mass exodus—our lowest point in numbers. The amount needed to build the prayer house was an unheard of amount for our church to give in one offering, even before so many people had left. By the end of the service our CPA totaled the offering and we announced to the whole church that we surpassed our goal by $8 and some change.

Testimonies. In the Old Testament the word testimony comes from the word, "do again." The implication is that God wants to repeat His wonderful works when we speak of what He has done. In the New Testament we have a confirmation of that principle in Revelation 19:10 (NASB): "*The testimony of Jesus is the spirit of prophecy.*" This says that if God has done it once, He is ready to do it again. The spoken or written record of whatever Jesus has done carries the prophetic anointing to cause a change in events in the spirit realm so that the miracle spoken of can happen again. Indeed, a testimony often carries the actual voice of the Lord. Learning to recognize it will enable us to accommodate and cooperate with the move of His Spirit that was released in the testimony.

One Sunday morning I was teaching about the power of a testimony and telling the story of a little boy that was healed of clubfeet. A family was visiting from out of state. They had a little girl, almost 2 years old, whose feet turned inward so severely that she would trip over her feet when she ran. The mother heard the testimony and said in her heart, "I'll take that for my daughter." When she picked up her little girl from our nursery, she noticed her feet were already perfectly straight! No one prayed for her. God spoke in the testimony, the mother heard, and the daughter was healed.

Senses. Our five senses are not only instruments that help us to enjoy life, they are tools that enable us to hear from God better. In the Psalms we are told that the songwriter's body actually hungered for God (see Ps. 84:2). In Hebrews, the writer states that the senses were to be *trained to discern good and evil* (see Heb. 5:14 NASB). In that passage, this ability is actually used as a mark of maturity—being able to use the senses to recognize God.

During one of our Sunday morning worship services, a young lady came and stood in front me. I sit on the end of the aisle, in the first row in the sanctuary. (The front of the auditorium fills up with people who want to give a more exuberant expression than you can do while stuck in the middle of a row.) As people raised their hands or danced with joy, she made all kinds of different motions with her hands and arms. We have quite a number of people involved in the occult who come to our meetings—some come out of hunger, some come to disturb. We don't make a big deal out of it, but we do stay on the alert.

I was puzzled by her and tried to discern what was going on. It was as though my discernment was shut off. But I did notice that it got cold where I was standing. I remembered a demonic encounter that my brother had several years earlier where his office turned very cold and remained so for several hours. So I walked about 15 feet away and noticed the temperature was normal. I went to Summer, who heads our prophetic dance ministry, and asked her to please go up on the stage and dance. I told her, "We need to break something." When she did, the young lady collapsed right in front of me. The demonic power that inspired her was broken through the prophetic act of the dance—*physical obedience brings spiritual release*. My wife knelt down next to her and brought deliverance to her and then led her to Christ.

CONNECTED TO ANOTHER WORLD

Having the heart and the ability to hear from God leaves us with an unlimited potential in resourcing earth with Heaven's resources. That connection to His world will prove necessary as we boldly invade the kingdoms of this world that are becoming the Kingdom of our Lord and Christ! That is the subject of the next chapter.

ENDNOTES

1. Many prominent authors and conference speakers add fuel to this fire of fear assuming that because the new age movement promotes it, its origins must be from the devil. I find that form of reasoning weak at best. If we follow that line of thought we will continue to give the devil the tools that God has given us for success in life and ministry. In doing so we will be building a confidence in the power of darkness above the Spirit of God.

2. We had many people in the revival of this hour speak to us in this way—"We know this is a move of God, it's just not for us." It's a shocking thing to see believers acknowledge God is among them, but watch them not respond to Him by crying out for more.

3. This is a phrase I use to describe *anticipating God to act or speak at any time.*

4. Cal Pierce, now of the Spokane Healing Rooms.

5. Kris Vallotton's Prophetic Manual, *A Call To War*, provides much practical instruction about this subject.

CHAPTER 5

Invading Babylon

*Any gospel that doesn't work
in the marketplace doesn't work.*

We have been given authority over this planet. It was first given to us in the commission God gave to mankind in Genesis (see Gen. 1:28-29). and was then restored to us by Jesus after His resurrection (see Matt. 28:18). But Kingdom authority is different than is typically understood by many believers. It is the authority to set people free from torment and disease, destroying the works of darkness. It is the authority to move the resources of Heaven through creative expression to meet human need. It is the authority to bring Heaven to earth. It is the authority to serve.

As with most Kingdom principles, the truths of humanity's dominion and authority are dangerous in the hands of those who desire to rule over others. These concepts seem to validate some people's selfishness. But when these truths are expressed through the humble servant, the world is rocked to its core. Becoming servants to this world is the key to open the doors of possibility that are generally thought of as closed or forbidden.

Neither our understanding of servants or of kings can help us much with this challenge for both are soiled in our world, probably beyond repair. That is where Jesus comes in. He is the King of all kings, yet the Servant of all. This unique combination found in the Son of God is the call of the hour upon us. As truth is usually found in the tension of two conflicting realities, we have an issue to solve. Like our Master we are both royalty and servants (see Rev. 1:5; Mark 10:45). Solomon warns of a potential problem, saying, *"the earth cannot bear up under a slave when he becomes king"* (Prov. 30:21-22 NASB). Yet Jesus contradicted Solomon's warning without nullifying the statement, by being effective at both. *Jesus served with the heart of a king, but ruled with the heart of a servant.* This is the essential combination that must be embraced by those longing to shape the course of history.

Royalty is my identity. Servanthood is my assignment. Intimacy with God is my life source. So, before God, I'm an intimate. Before people, I'm a servant. Before the powers of hell, I'm a ruler, with no tolerance for their influence. Wisdom knows which role to fulfill at the proper time.

INVADING THE MOUNTAINS OF INFLUENCE

There are seven realms of society that must come under the influence of the King and His Kingdom. For that to happen, we, as citizens of the Kingdom, must invade. The dominion of the Lord Jesus is manifest whenever the people of God go forth to serve by bringing the order and blessing of His world into this one.

The effort by many believers to simply obtain positions of leadership is putting the cart before the horse. Servanthood remains our strong suit, and it's through service that we can bring the benefits of His world into the reach of the common man.

The Kingdom is likened unto leaven (see Matt. 13:33). As yeast has an effect on the dough it is "worked into," so we will transform all the kingdoms of this world as we are worked into its systems.

From there we must display His dominion and rule. As the people of God move into these realms of society to show forth the benefits and values of the Kingdom, His government expands.

For this invasion to work effectively, we must correct a few misconceptions. In doing so, it is equally important to establish the necessary Kingdom principles in their proper order.

There is no such thing as secular employment for the believer. Once we are born again, everything about us is redeemed for Kingdom purposes. It is all spiritual. It is either a legitimate Kingdom expression, or we shouldn't be involved at all.

Every believer is in full-time ministry—only a few have pulpits in sanctuaries. The rest have their pulpit in their areas of expertise and favor in the world system. Be sure to preach only good news. And when necessary, use words!

The call of God is important, not because of the title it carries (or doesn't carry). It's valuable because of the One who called us. An assignment to be in business is as valuable in the Kingdom as is the call to be an evangelist. The privilege to be a stay-at-home wife and mother is equal in importance to being a missionary. Embrace your call with the faithfulness and thankfulness worthy of the One who has called you.

Our eternal rewards do not come because of how much money we made, how many souls were saved, or how many homeless people we fed. All rewards are given based on our faithfulness to what God has given and called us to be and to do. The honor we give to one another must not be only to those who have obvious spiritual occupations. Honor must be given to those who are faithful in the call, no matter what it is.

Prophetic ministry is not to be focused on the sins of the world. It takes very little discernment to find the dirt in people's lives. The prophetic in its purest form is designed to find the gold in people's lives and call it to the surface. This approach changes the attitude of the world toward the Church, and makes it possible for us to be contributors to society, not just confronters of all that is evil.

COVERT VS. OVERT MINISTRY

Our church and ministry school is most often known for it's overt ministry—outward and aggressive. We have seen hundreds of people healed and delivered in public places. We've even had words of knowledge[1] given over the intercom of a local grocery store. The results were amazing. People responded by gathering around cash register number 10 and received the healing ministry of Jesus through one of our young men named Chad. Following God's merciful display of power, they were invited to give their lives to Christ. Many did.

Overt ministry is very common for us. Whether it's in the mall, neighborhoods, schools, or places of business, the Gospel is brought to those in need. But this is only half of the needed ministry equation. The other half is covert ministry. The word *covert* means "hiding place." This refers to ministry that is more subtle in nature. It is hidden not because of cowardice but rather out of wisdom. It works within the systems of this world to bring about change by reestablishing the proper norms of thought, beliefs, disciplines, and relational boundaries. In other words, we work to change the culture. This requires more time, as the goal is not a specific healing or conversion. The goal is the transformation of society itself by invading the systems of the city in order to serve. Serving for their benefit, not ours, is the key. As someone once said, "*We shouldn't try to be the best in the world. We should try to be the best for the world!*" When we set aside our religious agendas to make others a success, we have learned the Kingdom mind-set, and have become a part of the transformation movement.

DUMPING RELIGIOUS AGENDAS

The Church is sometimes known for its willingness to serve, but usually with well-meaning spiritual agendas as the ultimate goal. It almost sounds blasphemous, but serving simply to get people saved is a religious agenda. As pure and noble as it may seem to us as believers, it is manipulative to the world, and is viewed as impure service. The world can smell it a mile away. We put them on the defensive when we carry such reasons for serving into their sphere of responsibility. But, for example, when we volunteer in our local school to help the principal succeed, then we've crossed the line into territory seldom visited by the Church. It is serving for the benefit of another. It's that kind of a servant that the world welcomes. The amazing bonus is you also end up influencing the school in ways you never thought possible, including bringing people to Christ.

What would happen if parents volunteered in their local schools to help the teacher succeed? Generally teachers have an authentic interest in children succeeding in life. They invest themselves for the sake of another generation. They deserve honor for their commitment; and we can help them succeed.

School districts are accustomed to Christians seeking positions on local school boards. Sometimes parents will work with another parent to get a principal to fire a teacher because they're an atheist, or to change a particular curriculum. But what would happen if we actually invaded the systems of this world to give honor where it is due instead of dishonor those whom we think deserve expulsion? The former brings transformation through favor. The latter is a self-fulfilling prophecy of rejection as the world has few options but to protect what they are stewards over from the *outside group* (us) that wants to be in control. Christians are notorious for trying to take over schools through political maneuvering.[2] It may work from time to time, but it is not Kingdom. Nor is it long-lasting. There is a better way.

Interestingly enough, the fullness of the Spirit can also be seen in these two distinct approaches to ministry. As stated in Chapter 2, the fullness of the Spirit makes way for "believers that walk in wisdom, making practical contributions to the needs of society, who also confront the impossibilities of life through the provisions of the Cross—solutions through supernatural display. Perhaps it is these two things working in tandem that should be considered *the balanced Christian life.*"

THE SEVEN MIND-MOLDERS OF SOCIETY

Both Dr. Bill Bright, founder of Campus Crusade for Christ, and Loren Cunningham, founder of Youth With A Mission, received the same revelation from God around the same period of time: there are seven major realms of influence in society that shape the way we live and think. These mountains of influence must be invaded by Kingdom-oriented people for the transformation of society to take place. These mountains are:

- Home.
- Church.
- Education.
- Media (Electronic and Print).
- Government & Politics.
- Performing Arts (including Entertainment and Sports).
- Commerce (including Science and Technology).

It is interesting to note that God gave this insight to two men who lead significant youth movements. It is obvious that God wants an entire generation to value their call regardless of what title it brings, teaching them how to invade a culture for its total and complete transformation. God fully intends for there to be a fulfillment of His Word about *"the kingdoms of this world have become the kingdoms of our Lord"* (Rev. 11:15).

The following list is a little different from the original. It is not an improved list, but it does have a slightly different emphasis to more accurately represent our application of these principles. They are: *Business, Education, the Church, Family, Arts/ Entertainment, Science & Medicine, and Government* (not listed in any order of importance).

Wisdom is the vital ingredient to be effective in this invasion. As a reminder, we've defined wisdom with these three words: Integrity, Creativity, and Excellence. It is the display of the mind of God, always in the context of integrity that brings forth the creative solutions for life while holding to the standards of excellence. These play a vital role in manifesting the Kingdom in ways that honor God and solve the issues of life for humankind.

BUSINESS

Many Christians have tried to gain favor and position in the business world, but have failed miserably. It is hard to gain favor in that world without prosperity. Prosperity is a primary measure for success in that arena. With that in mind, the world is also full of stories of great financial success that were disasters in every other way. People instinctively want both—outward and inward success. The Kingdom businessperson has the chance to display a more complete picture of success by focusing not only on money. Their celebration of life, with all its many facets, will grab the attention of those hopelessly trapped in the "money is success" daily grind.

While there is room for overt ministry in every part of life, it is generally not the outward preaching of the Gospel that secures the place of favor in the eyes of the unbelieving businessperson. It is divine order (Kingdom) in the overall approach to life—to self, family, business, and community.

Even the world knows that money is not the only measure of true success. Most of those in business want much more than money for their labors. Simple things like joy, a happy home life, recognition, and meaningful friendships are an important part of the life of true prosperity. John, the Beloved, referred to this as "prosperity of soul" (see 3 John 2). Mixed into this quest is the cry for significance. The Kingdom businessperson is poised to illustrate that element by their approach to life. The extra efforts in world relief, along with the personal participation in helping the poor of our own cities as well as other projects requiring giving and sacrifice, help to give definition for the favor of God that is upon the Kingdom businessperson.

One of our men sold cars at a local used car lot owned by believers. When a woman came in to buy a car, he noticed that she was very troubled. Through the direction of the Holy Spirit, he was able to minister to her quite profoundly. She opened up to God and received major healing in her heart. When they were through he told her, "Because you have opened up your heart to me, I cannot sell you a car. It would be unfair for me to do so. Instead I will introduce you to another salesman who will help you find the kind of car you are looking for." He was unwilling to come close to the possibility of taking advantage of this woman by selling her something when she had become emotionally vulnerable to him.

Kris Vallotton used to own an automobile repair shop and several car part stores. A man once stole some tires and rims from his shop. However, he didn't realize that Kris knew he was the thief, and brought his car in to Kris' repair shop. When that customer came in to pick up his car and pay his bill, Kris took him into his office and told him, "I know you stole my tires and rims. And to show you that I forgive you I am giving you the work we did on your truck for free." The man went to his vehicle and sat in silence for about five minutes without doing anything, just staring off into space. (Occasionally, a person receives a Gospel tract that they will never forget. This man received one stamped "Paid in Full.")

Then there is the humorous story of an employee wanting to get one of his workmates in trouble. He told his boss, "Every time I pass his office he's just staring out the window. He needs to be fired!" His boss responded, "Leave him alone! Just the other day he came up with an idea that saved us over $300,000—by just staring out that window."

Creativity is a necessary component for the Kingdom businessperson. It brings fresh ideas that keep adventure as a central part of their assignment. Witty inventions are going to increase in the

Christian community, as God is using that expression of wisdom to bring about a transfer of wealth for Kingdom purposes.

"Do you see a man who excels in his work? He will stand before kings; He will not stand before unknown men" (Prov. 22:29). This verse tells us two things: One, the result of lives pursuing excellence; they will influence the influencers. Two, kings demand excellence. Many compromise in this area to make a quick buck, but it is excellence that provides wealth for the long term. It's a wealth that has no sorrow (see Prov. 10:22). Excellence is a Kingdom value, and is not to be confused with perfectionism, which is a counterfeit and comes from the religious spirit. One of the clearest paths of promotion is through excellence.

EDUCATION

Often times the Church reacts to the abuses of the world system and creates an error equal in danger to one we've rejected. This was never truer than in the realm of education. The Western mind-set, that values reason as the only proper measure of truth, has undermined the Gospel. This worldview, which Paul battled in First Corinthians, has been embraced by our educational culture. It is anti-Christ in nature. The supernatural then becomes subject to the evaluation of ignorant people. But the solution to this problem is not to reject education; the answer is to invade. Our rejection removes us from our place of preservation as *the salt of the earth* (Matt.5:13).

God is willing to debate anyone (see Isa. 1:18). He is very secure in His understanding and arguments. He also backs up His insights with evidence that will bear up under scrutiny. Invading the educational system is essential as it's this mountain that greatly shapes the minds and expectations of the younger generation. While it could be argued that today entertainers have a greater role in shaping the minds of the young, it is the educators who generally shape the minds of the entertainers in their way of thinking.

Our young people need to believe they will be able to live their entire lives on this earth, and plan accordingly. Get educated, married, have children, all with a Kingdom mind-set. Too many generations who experience the outpouring of the Spirit forfeit their desires for training and education in order to do "the Lord's work." As noble as that sounds, it comes from a misunderstanding of real ministry aided by the idea that we will be taken out of here at any moment. This is a tender subject, as we must be ready to be with the Lord at any given moment. But, as the Church regains the value for *no job is secular for the believer*, the esteem will return for the positions in society that had little value in prior generations. The desire for Heaven is right and healthy. But it must not replace our commission; "*Your kingdom come. Your will be done, on earth as it is in heaven*" (Matt. 6:10 NASB). We were not commissioned to look into the clouds for His coming (see Acts 1:11). We were commanded to "occupy" until He comes (Luke 19:13 KJV). *Occupy* is a military term. And according to Kingdom values, occupation is always for the purpose of advancement.

Our children must become educated, and become educators. But that goal is not complete without the Kingdom mind-set. We are sending them into dangerous territory to get their training. Choose their schools carefully. Each teacher that trains your child is a delegated authority—delegated by you. The Bible does not give the authority for training children to the government, no matter how noble their intent. It rests upon your shoulders, so pray, pray, pray, and educate, educate, educate.

We would never send our child to a restaurant where only one in ten die of food poisoning. Yet we do that daily in our educational system, with odds that are much worse than one in ten. We often send them out, unguarded, into a system that works to undermine faith and ultimately their relationship with God. The answer is not to withdraw from society and move into the mountains to preserve the family unit. The answer is to train and invade. Our training is superior to theirs if it's authentic, because it is driven by a personal relationship with God, and includes transforming divine encounters.

As for the believers who are already in the educational system, bravo! Invade with a Kingdom mind-set. Such a way of thinking provides the mooring needed to stay stable in storms and conflict. It also puts you in place to provide the answers to the dilemmas created by the inferior "Greek" mind-set. Most bad ideas (including bad theology) are only one divine encounter away from oblivion. We owe people an encounter with God. And that is what you carry into that mountain of influence.

Most people in our culture unknowingly live under the influence of a dark kingdom. Yet they suffer with problems that have their answer in the Kingdom of God and the believer. Both wisdom and power are available to us that we might provide solutions from another world that meet their needs.

At Bethel Church, we have a waiting list of schools wanting us to be part of their after-school program. Why? We have come alongside to serve, not take over. The liberty that is given to our teams (presently seven schools a week) is really quite amazing. There are many who believe that what we are doing is impossible. And as long as the Church maintains an adversarial relationship with the educational system, it will remain impossible.

Throughout Scripture we see that when God's people step forward to serve, God backs it up with power. The schools are asking for our help. They face problems on a daily basis that were unheard of 30 years ago. It is our hour to invade, serve, and shine for His glory!

Moral values are the basis for integrity. And moral values are rooted in the character of God. The supernatural educator has access to a realm of stability that others don't have. That is not to say one has to be a believer to have integrity. Many unbelievers do. But the supernatural element available in the realm of character is reserved for those who have the Spirit of the resurrected Christ living in them. Young people need educators with integrity, but they also need those who believe in them. Calling out the treasure in a young person can mark them for good forever. Often times such an educator plants a seed that another person will harvest, but that is the joy of this Kingdom—no words return void. (See 1 Cor. 3:5-9 and Isa. 55:11.)

We have a team of educators in our church who, through Kingdom principles, have tapped into ways of defeating learning disorders in many children. This creative expression came to them through divine inspiration. It is the result of people realizing they have legal access into the mysteries of the Kingdom, and have a responsibility to bring those secrets into play in the lives of those with great needs. This affects all the lives within their sphere of influence. There are answers to every problem we face. There are methods of training people that are far superior to what we know now. Kingdom-oriented people, who know who they are in Christ, will access these secrets for the benefit of all who are around them.

Excellence is more than exhorting students to get good grades. It is a gift from God that uses the full measure of resources from both the natural and spiritual realities. Some just seem to be good at everything, while others appear to have been absent the day gifts and talents were given out. In reality, each person has an area where God has gifted them to excel and it's the wise educator who discovers that area in a child. An excellent teacher will bring excellence out of the one who can't find it in themselves.

ENTERTAINMENT

Entertainment includes the arts, professional sports, and the media.

It wasn't too long ago that the world of entertainment was deemed so unholy that believers were forbidden to enter. The Church has often fallen to the notion that darkness is stronger than light. Entertainment is a mountain of influence that must be invaded.

The indictment of that realm being 'unholy' was accurate, but unfortunately, it is also a self-fulfilling prophecy—anywhere we do not invade becomes darker in our absence. We are the *"light of the world"* (Matt. 5:14). The realms of society that we fail to invade are hopelessly lost to darkness. Invasion is the responsibility of light.

This is a realm which ought to have edification as a primary objective. When it is perverted, it steals and plunders. But in its primary function, it creates. Recreation comes from this—re-creation! It must not only be creative, it must create.

Heaven has what we want. Every creative dream is fulfilled in Heaven. The great news is that we have access to that realm through prayers of faith. For example: there are sounds in Heaven that earth has never heard. When a musician taps into that reality and communicates that sound here, Heaven will have found agreement and will invade. All art finds its origins in the person of God; more specifically, it's found in His holiness. The Scripture says, *"in the beauty of holiness"* (Ps. 29:2).   It's tragic that holiness gets such poor treatment from the people of God. It is God's nature, His person. Beauty pours forth from that one attribute (see 2 Chron. 20:21).

When I was growing up there were few Christians in this mountain of influence. Baseball was my love, and I only knew of two Christians in all of baseball. I'm sure there were more, but the point is it wasn't common. Today there are many teams that have a large percentage of genuine believers. The same is true of the arts. No field is left untouched. God is planting His last days' army in these strategic places of influence.

Mel Gibson's movie *The Passion of the Christ* is testimony to the turning that is taking place in this mountain. The doors of this realm are open wide, as creativity is at an all-time low. Immorality, jealousy, hatred, and revenge are poor substitutes for real creativity.

There's such a vacuum in the area of integrity in this mountain that all true Kingdom people will quickly stand out. However, we can't be nonchalant about the pressure to conform to worldly standards that the believer will face. Being a stumbling block to others has been become an art form for many. People receive justification for their own immoral lifestyles by getting others to fall morally. But for those who have true foundations, the sky is the limit. In crisis, people will always turn to those who are stable. Integrity will be a beacon of light to those wandering through this land of disappointment and shame.

It might seem that creativity is where we have the biggest challenge in this mountain of influence. The opposite is true. Writers, designers, and the like have substituted sensuality for creativity. This has left a huge gap in the area of real originality. Anyone who has escaped the pressure to duplicate trash will automatically be positioned to create. Learning how to pray in the Spirit and *soak* in His presence will give great advantages to those wanting to invade this mountain. Heaven has what we're looking for. And you'll have to go there to get it. The best novels and plays have yet to be written. The most beautiful melodies to ever grace the human ear are yet to be discovered. Those with an ear for God, discovering the experience of "being seated in heavenly places" will have access to things no other generation has ever seen before.

Many have mistakenly thought that the devil has all the good music. He is not creative. Tragically, he receives credit for too many things, even by the Church. How is it that an ungodly person can write a beautiful piece of music, or a brilliant script for a movie? How is it they can paint a masterpiece or design buildings that take our breath away? They were made in the image of God, and He doesn't remove that distinguishing feature when a person rebels against Him (see Rom. 11:29). In recent days, believers who have adopted the Kingdom mind-set have caught up to, and in some cases surpassed, the world in the area of excellence and will continue to do so.

THE CHURCH

Jesus gave His disciples a warning about the potential influence of religion on the mind, saying, "*Beware of the leaven of the Pharisees and the leaven of Herod*" (Mark 8:15). The mentality of the Pharisee places God at the center of everything, but He's impersonal and powerless. Their God dwells mostly in the realm of theory and supposition. They excel at traditions that are convenient, and reverence that is self-serving. But there's not much in the religious community that is actually Kingdom. It has a wide-open door for people with a renewed mind.

Many in the religious community have a lot of sincerity. And when they see someone who actually practices the purity and power from the pages of Scripture, something comes alive in them. They hope it's true. They just lack examples. Kingdom-oriented people have great opportunities in the midst of great opposition. But the rewards are worth every risk.

Success is often measured by numbers of people attending services, copies of books or CDs sold, or how many watch their TV show. One of the most common fears in this world of influence is that "someone will steal my sheep." Being committed to another leader's success, with no personal agenda for gain, is essential for invasion into this mountain. Ignoring the external measurements of success will enable the leader in this realm to value what the King values—passion, purity, power, and people.

Compassion is one of the greatest tools we possess to invade this mountain of influence. One of the churches in our network wanted to touch a local Catholic orphanage. They live in a country where Protestants and Catholics do not work together. In fact, they are known for preaching against the one another from their pulpits. When the pastor went to the priest to talk, the priest was naturally guarded. Yet the pastor worked hard to share with him that they wanted the opportunity to honor them for their heart for the orphans. He noted that they were doing something important that none of the Protestants had been willing to do. The pastor asked if there was anything the children needed. The priest told them of their need for shoes. In spite of their very limited resources, the Protestant church bought shoes for each child. The sacrifice needed for this particular church family to do such a thing is beyond what I can write about on these pages. Yet they did. From this simple act of love, the entire Church in this region has been rocked by this display of an authentic Gospel. And a city is being healed from the religious animosity that has ruled over that area for decades.

The area of morality and integrity should be the area in which we have little problem. But that is not the case. While I don't believe the statistics that claim the Church (authentic believers) is equal to the world in divorce and immorality, the numbers are admittedly far too high. Divine encounters, accurate teaching from Scripture, and accountability to other members of the Body can help change this problem. Righteous people can provide a righteous peer pressure. When fellowship becomes valuable enough that it is sacrificial, then those in fellowship begin to walk in the light—openly, with integrity and accountability. (See Heb. 13:15-16.)

The Church is known for its ruts, not its new ideas. Thankfully a great transformation is taking place in that area. While change for change's sake is not always healthy, those resistant to change are usually resistant to the Holy Spirit. If anyone should be known for creativity, it should be those in whom the accurate image of the Creator has been formed—born-again believers. There are better ways of doing things. Always. And the Church is in the place of leading the way. Cultural relevance is rightfully the cry of the hour, but it must be relevance *with* power!

The Church has often taken the low road in the realm of excellence because of a misunderstanding of humility. But the choice of that road usually flows from low faith, and humility gets the blame. Excellence can and must be the expression of true humility as humility declares, "Our best, for His glory!" Most of the areas that can bring the greatest results have the greatest risk. This is no exception. Excellence is Kingdom. Perfectionism is religion. Poverty is demonic.

FAMILY

The pressure being exerted on the family today makes this one of the easiest and most important areas to invade. Even those who seem to work overtime to destroy the family unit, instinctively hunger for healthy relationships, significance, and a legacy. All a family needs to do to have influence in this mountain is to be healthy, and not hidden. When relationships are good and the boundaries of godly disciplines are intact, there is no limit to the influence of the Christian home. The problem has often been a false standard of holiness wherein the Christian doesn't associate with the unbeliever, yet maintains similar values and habits to them. The opposite should be our goal—mingle and associate with the lost, but don't take on their values or habits. That way we, as both salt and light, have our proper effect of preserving and exposing in order to bring them into their destiny. Healthy families that are intentional, breed healthy families.

One of our local high schools was having a problem with some of their students. Some parents had lost control of their kids and were clueless as to what to do. The school was considering removing these students permanently from their program. The principal recognized an unusual gift for family life in a couple of our pastors. Their heart was not to dominate or take over; they simply wanted to serve. The principal took a huge risk and asked them to come and mentor these parents about functional home life. The transformation within the families' relationships was amazing. Teenagers who had previously cursed their parents to their face were suggesting the whole family play a board game before they all went to bed. Some of them requested a regular time to talk each evening. The turnaround was so astonishing that there is a waiting list of public schools that want this team to come and work with their parents.

When parents have godly character and wisdom for raising children, they produce a family that reflects the love and integrity of Christ. If children grow up seeing one standard in church and another at home, they tend to rebel against standards all together. Conversely, when integrity is genuine both in and out of the public eye, children grow up willing to pay the price needed to follow in their parents' footsteps, as long as they have been given room for individuality.

This is one area where an ounce of effort translates into a pound of impact. Few families actually purposely live the adventure of life together. Embracing such an adventure together is what gives place for creative expression to surface. My wife has been so good for our household in this area. She is adventurous by nature and tends to add joy to the things I might unintentionally crush by my intensity. I learned from her, because I wanted to learn. My family is better…and I am better, because of her quest for creativity in the home.

This simply means that we always do things to the best of our ability. Sometimes money is tight. Excellence can't be measured in buying the finest car or the most expensive clothes. Rather it is displayed in our approach to life—all of us, for all of Him. It's a great deal!!

GOVERNMENT

Knowing that Jesus is the "desire of the nations" encourages us as we approach this mountain of influence. It means our simple task is to make the desired One visible.

Government usually lives in a crippled state because of the fear of voters. Noble people enter that world and end up loosing their dreams on the altar of intimidation. The *leaven of Herod* poisons many (see Mark 8:15). But there is a new breed being groomed for this hour who fears only God and lives with a wisdom that enables one to dance through the minefield of public opinion. Such is the price of working effectively in government.

Those who climb this mountain of influence must realize that it is necessary to increase "*in favor with God and men*" (Luke 2:52), just as Jesus did. Proverbs is probably the most practical book of instruction on this subject. Reading a chapter a day, according to the date, will give leaders in this realm a compass bearing so that no issue arises that doesn't have a Kingdom solution.

One of the women in our congregation was recently working in an Arab country for the U.S. State Department. She was invited to give input into the educational system in that country. They had a problem with the discipline of high school boys, and though they rarely empower women in their country at that level, the favor upon her life was larger than the cultural barrier. She addressed the instructors and then wrote a paper on the subject, based on the principles we live by in our church—all Kingdom principles of discipline. Their educational leaders were so impressed with the report that they adopted it as the standard of discipline for their school system for the entire nation. The U.S. embassy responded in like manner, sending the report to their embassies around the world.

It is unfortunate that the words *integrity* and *politician* are considered an oxymoron. The Word of God remains true—*"when it goes well with the righteous, the city rejoices"* (Prov. 11:10). People instinctively want to be governed by people who are honest and righteous. They want leaders who are not self-serving, but will actually govern sacrificially for the benefit of the whole. Here again is where we need to embrace the standard of Jesus, which is to serve like a king and rule like a servant. It is His way.

It is sad to see believers who fall to the political tactics of unbelieving opponents because their popularity has declined in the public opinion polls. There are better ways of doing things, from running a campaign to surrounding oneself with people of wisdom for good decisions. All of these things are marks of a person committed to the wisdom of creativity.

Two of the most basic roles of government are to create a realm of safety and a realm of prosperity. When governmental leaders use their position for personal gain, it amounts to prostituting their charisma for themselves. Excellence is found in doing our best for the sake of others.

SCIENCE & MEDICINE

This is becoming a bigger influence in the world all the time. Diseases are on the increase, with little sign of cures. I believe in divine healing and have seen thousands healed through Jesus Christ, but I'm not opposed to medical intervention. The entire medical community is gaining power, credibility, and influence throughout our society.

One of our ministry targets is to pray for all those who are with the dying. That includes doctors and nurses, ambulance workers, convalescent hospital employees, police, firefighters, etc. We are praying that the righteous are assigned to those places of influence, because we want to make it nearly impossible to get to hell from our city.

We have a person in a place of authority in one of the convalescent hospitals in our area. It is written on the medical charts that the nurses must call her when anyone is dying so she can be with them. If necessary she will even remove the family members from that patient for a few minutes while she prays with them to receive Christ. We don't want people politely going to hell from our city. You've heard the saying; *there are no atheists in foxholes*—the same could be said of those on the edge of eternity. People are very receptive to the Truth when they are facing death. Authentic love and compassion for people, expressed by those planted within that system, brings forth a wonderful harvest. It's amazing what we are allowed to do when we go in low just to serve. People know the difference between authentic love and a person fulfilling their religious obligations. Real love has very few opponents.

Christ-like character always puts others first. This highly respected industry has fallen on hard times due to the great number of doctors who make questionable decisions based on profit margins.

Hospitals are often in the crosshairs of critics as they often operate without compassion. Yet that is not the norm. Most of those in this profession at least started out with sincere compassion and a desire to help others. Kingdom-oriented people will once again be easy to spot as the need is so great. And if those individuals believe in the power of God to heal, all the better. Miracles occur through the hands of medical professionals at an increasing rate. The number of doctors who attend our healing conferences is growing dramatically. It's a beautiful combination when we see a whole segment of society raised up that can work in both the natural and the supernatural realms to bring about good health.

More and more Christian doctors are being trained by God to find answers to health issues. As wonderful as healing is, divine health is greater. Believers have been given access to the mysteries of the Kingdom regarding this subject. It would be tragic to come to the end of time and have the only generation to experience divine health be the Israelites. They lived under an inferior covenant and were in rebellion against God. Inferior covenants cannot make superior promises. Those in this mountain of influence have access to things that the entire world is aggressively asking for. Asking God for specific solutions will enable those involved in medicine to give true creative expression to a dying world.

This group of professionals has a head start in the area of excellence, as they are accustomed to paying a significant price for their role in society. If they can maintain passion and discipline, while embracing a humble heart, nothing will be impossible for them.

Passion for God Creates Passion for Other Things

Keeping passionate and encouraged is vital while facing the privilege of ascending these mountains of influence. Passion wears out when it relies solely on self-motivation. God has fire in His eyes! Frequent encounters with Him will keep any flame in us burning. But encouragement is another matter. *"One who speaks in a tongue edifies himself* (1 Cor. 14:4 NASB). Dr. Lance Wallnau adds an interesting twist to this word *edifies*. He points out that *edifice* is a related word, and that one who prays in tongues *builds the edifice from which the purposes of God for their life becomes manifest!* Perhaps this is why the apostle Paul claimed that he spoke in tongues more than anyone else. He was building something big for God!

We often still think in terms of spiritual and secular, thus eliminating our influence in areas that are not overtly spiritual. This next chapter will deal with the practical application of these truths and expand on this concept of *how our love for God affects our love for other things.*

ENDNOTES

1. A word of knowledge is when a person knows something about someone else that they couldn't know without God revealing it to them. In this case, it was knowing about specific illnesses of those shopping in that store whom God wanted to heal.

2. Being involved in the political process is not only acceptable for the believer, it is essential. We just cannot lower our standards by thinking that our strength is in the political process. Natural efforts in obedience to God bring spiritual release. His invasion is our strength.

CHAPTER 6

The Practical Side of Things

If it matters to you, it matters to Him.

Perhaps you've heard it said, *God is number one, the family is number two, and the Church is number three....* That unofficial list is important as it outlines a few of the priorities in a Christian's life that have become confused through the years. I know of many tragedies in pastor's families because they ignored these priorities of Kingdom living. Yet, as good as this list is, I don't believe it is technically accurate. When God is number one, there is no number two.

Out of my love for God I give myself to my wife and kids. It's not separate from the Lord, but is unto Him. It's not that I can't love my wife without loving God—many unbelievers do that well. But in knowing and loving God, I am released to a measure of supernatural love that is unattainable apart from God. It should be said that anyone who is completely abandoned to God should love others more than they thought possible. It is because of my passion for Jesus that I love the Church the way I do. My love for God *is* my love for life. They cannot be separated. Loving my family, church, ministry…is an expression of my love for God. God being number one, the only One.

Religion is what destroys this process because it implies that only overtly spiritual activities are acceptable as service to God and that anything that doesn't have to do with Bible reading, witnessing, church attendance, etc. is not true Christian service. Religion takes us back to the concept of spiritual and secular parts of the Christian life. The person living this dual life needs a list of priorities to survive; otherwise they will not take care of other matters of importance. Their concept of God doesn't allow them to actually have a passion for something that is not viewed as a Christian discipline.

What may appear to be semantics for some has purpose for this reason: we must have a shift in thinking whereby we recognize that passion for God *gives birth* to a passion for other things. And it's those other things that are often to be pursued *as unto the Lord*. We shouldn't experience them as something in competition with, or separate from our devotion to God. Perhaps the best example of this in Scripture is found in First John 4:20. It says that if we love God it will be measurable by our love for people. This is such an absolute principle that God says if we don't love others, we don't actually love Him. The point is this: in the wake of our passion for God, passion for other things is created. It is often in giving ourselves to those things that we prove and manifest our love for God.

In my case my love of the outdoors is part of my devotion to Christ. While some worship nature, I worship the One it points to—the Creator. My love for my family, for hunting and fishing, the mountains and the ocean, fountain pens, and French roast coffee, are all part of the enjoyment of life for me; and that joy is born completely through a relationship with Him.

The heavens are telling of the glory of God; and their expanse is declaring the work of His hands. Day to day pours forth speech, and night to night reveals knowledge (Psalms 19:1-2 NASB).

For since the creation of the world His invisible attributes, His eternal power and divine nature, have been clearly seen, being understood through what has been made, so that they are without excuse (Romans 1:20 NASB).

DAVID'S CHIEF JOY

Throughout Scripture David is known as "the man after God's heart." His passion for God seems unparalleled in Scripture; yet he also illustrates a love for life that is without equal. In Psalms 137:6 (NASB), he says, "*May my tongue cling to the roof of my mouth if I do not remember you, if I do not exalt Jerusalem above my chief joy.*" In today's religious community this statement would probably not be accepted. How can Jerusalem, the community of the redeemed, be called his chief joy? Isn't God supposed to be his chief joy? The apparent paradox fits perfectly into the Jewish culture that looks for practical expression of spiritual truths. David's love for God needed expression, and Jerusalem was a perfect target.

When we live with genuine passion for God, it creates a passion for other things. *While it is possible to value other things above God, it is not possible to value God without valuing other things.* This is the key point confronting the religious mindset, which dismisses everything not considered sacred. The effort to accomplish the goal of loving God with no other passions has had to create a monastic lifestyle to survive. And while I admire many of the monastic believers in the past, it is not the model that Jesus gave us. The way we steward the rest of life becomes the litmus test that demonstrates an authentic love for God.

MY PRIORITIES VS. GOD'S

Like most people, I have a list of things I pray for. They represent the basic desires and needs of my life and those I love. If they're not written down on paper, they're at least written in my heart. On the list are things which have obvious eternal significance—prayer for our cities, for the salvation of certain people we've ministered to, for healing breakthrough in tough cases, provision—both personal and the church. Following the urgent is the "it would be nice" section of the list. It is long and has varying degrees of importance. But I've noticed that God sometimes bypasses the list and goes directly to the "I haven't even bothered to ask" part that dwells somewhere deep in my heart. It is a pleasant and sometimes offensive move.

On one such occasion a friend came up to me and said, "Hey, would you like a hunting dog?" I've always wanted to have a well-trained hunting dog, but never had the time or money for such a luxury. Nor was it on my list. He went on to say, "A dog trainer owes me a big favor and said he'd get me any kind of dog I want. I don't need another dog. So tell me what kind of dog you'd like and I'll get it for you." Just like that, I was to be the owner of a dog that wasn't on my prayer list. It wasn't even on the "it would be nice" part of my list. It wasn't important enough. It was, however, a secret desire in my heart. God bypassed all the stuff that had such eternal significance and went to something temporal and seemingly insignificant.

It offended me at first. Not that I wasn't thankful; I was. But it made no sense. I would have preferred He let me use that *trump card* for something that is more important to me.

It took awhile, but eventually I got it. My requests were important, but my view of Him was more important. It was then and there I started to see that *if it matters to me, it matters to Him*. His bypassing my "urgent" prayer list, my "it would be nice" list, and entering the "secret desires of the heart" list told me more about my heavenly Father than answering all the other things I had been praying about.

A RESTORED VIEW OF PRAYER

People frequently come asking me to pray with them for someone else's healing. Sometimes they have an obvious physical need themselves, but will ask for their friend's healing instead. When I press them about their own condition, they usually say something like, "Oh, I'd rather have God heal them than me. They have cancer. I only have a ruptured disc in my back." Their compassion is wonderful because they are putting another person's need before their own. But their concept of God is wrong. Really wrong!

He doesn't have limited power. In other words, He won't run out of power after He heals their back. He'll still have enough power left to heal their friend's cancer. Also, you don't just get one wish and run out after the first one is used up. The desire for a friend is noble, but it's not an "either/or" situation. Besides that, His attention span is excellent; so good in fact that He can give His undivided attention to every human being on the planet, all at the same time. Neither does He view our prayers on the same priority scale that we do. Some would see it this way: "Of course God heals cancer. That's important. My ruptured disc is not as important. I have learned to live with it." We think of cancer being urgent (which it is) and everything else should be put on hold. In reality, it's often the blown disc that gets healed first. And the increase of faith in that one experience helps to bring about the faith needed for healing of the cancer. Our logic is not consistent with His, and He isn't going to change.

DREAMS THAT MATTER

In this chapter I bring to you three stories, and an unusual experience in a hotel. They are true, simple, and yet profound. Out of the hundreds of stories that could be written, I chose these because they have no obvious eternal significance in themselves. Yet they are rife with meaning for those wanting to impact their world. The reports of God invading governments and various systems of the world to bring change are increasing daily. Many are included in other wonderful books. While they have great importance for us, for me, the nature of God is seen more clearly in His answer for the simple, temporal things.

TOXIC FURNITURE POLISH

Barry & Julie Schaffer had a wood finishing company, which they opened in 1987. They pre-finish woodwork for homes and commercial properties. The materials they used were toxic and quite hazardous. They were concerned for all the obvious reasons and began to search for a high-quality, water-based product. They decided that if they couldn't find a good water-based product to use they would quit the industry. The search was on, yet nothing they tried had the same quality as the toxic materials they were using.

After several years of working with products that did not work well, they decided to try to develop one themselves. Barry contacted people in the business as well as get formulas from chemical companies. He tried over and over to work with what they told him but nothing looked right or worked well.

After the tragic death of their third child, Amy, Julie and Barry came to know Jesus. Once again we see the wonderful grace of God to use the very thing sent to destroy us to actually bring us to Him. Following their conversion, Julie still had several miscarriages. She became pregnant with their fourth child but began to bleed. She told Barry that she would not be back to work until she knew that they were going to have this baby. Julie went home to pray and seek the Lord for as long as it would take. Each day Barry would come home to make lunch for her. She didn't leave the couch for almost two months. They prayed each day, and then he would return to work. On one of those days they began to pray and the Holy Spirit gave Julie a sequence of letters and numbers with instructions to tell Barry. She was hesitant, feeling very awkward since this had never happened before. When she did, he said, "I think I know what that means." He went back to their shop and used it as the formula for making the topcoat that he had been trying to make for years. It worked! He used this formula to manufacture their non-toxic, water-based product for the next several years. The same formula became the foundation for many other products.

They always gave God all the glory for their radical conversion, and this creative idea. They also believed that God would receive even more glory if things would continue to develop, and tried many times to expand their business. Neither of them had the time, money, or ambition to pursue the big marketing arena. Then, in 2001, a man built a log home in upper Michigan, and used their products. He was a 44-year-old retired businessman who had made a lot of money in the computer industry. He used their stains and finishes on the interior of his home and was so impressed that he talked to the contractor about them. When he heard that they were a small town company, owned and operated by two people, his entrepreneurial mind was activated. He contacted them about selling the company. They prayed and prayed about this because they knew God had given it to them. After two years of seeking the Lord they agreed to discuss a possible sale. When they finally agreed on an amount, it was more than they could have imagined making in their entire lifetime. They agreed to sell the company to begin a new life of serving the Lord in missions and in evangelism.

It was God's creative ability that brought these things to pass. Barry doesn't hold a chemistry degree. He prayed whenever he got stuck in the creative process, and God always had the right person call or the right sample show up. The major breakthrough came when the "Holy Spirit impressions" that Julie had actually contained a formula for the ultimate product—a mystery contained in the Kingdom realm, but out of reach until it was sought after.

For them, the greatest miracle of all followed. After being told they would never have another child, the Lord gave them their fourth, a son.

A BETTER BOW

Matt McPherson is known as a man with great passion for God. His love is to minister the Gospel through music and leading in worship. However, after being handed a $15 check for a weekend of ministry, he realized that it would be a very challenging way to support his family. Soon after that experience, the Lord gave him this wonderful promise: I am going to prosper you in business, so you can be self-sufficient in ministry. The following is a brief report of God's faithfulness to that promise.

Matt's approach to life is refreshing, as he is bothered by mediocrity. The thought of being average is frightening. He has no desire for fame or power, but refuses to be passive with his life. He wants to make a difference. His love for God has created a passion for excellence and creativity that is admirable.

One day God spoke something to him that would forever change his life. He said, I know every answer to every problem in the world. If men would only ask me, I would give them the answers. Matt was overwhelmed with the promise and the sense of awe he had for God in that moment. He dropped to his knees and cried out to God about the things that concerned him. As a young man Matt developed a hobby of making and shooting compound bows. He obtained the love of archery grew while hunting with his father and brothers in his early years. Following the revelation about God having the answers to every issue in life, he asked God about how to build a better bow. He knew hundreds of ways not to build one, but wanted to take God's invitation to ask for answers for any problem. Several weeks later, at around three o'clock in the morning, he woke up seeing a piece of paper suspended before his eyes. It looked as though it was torn from a notebook. On it was a sketch of a compound bow, revealing a new concept. When his wife, Sherry, asked him what he was doing, he said, "I think I'm having a vision." He was. In response to his prayer, God gave him the initial concept for what would eventually launch the Mathews Archery Company, changing the archery industry forever.

Compound bows have an intrinsic problem to them: they have two cams/pulleys that must be properly synchronized to get the bow to work correctly. The idea that God put on the suspended sheet of paper was a whole new concept in bow design. It was a single-cam bow that eliminated the synchronizing issues. This idea alone turned the archery industry upside down.

Today, Mathews Inc. is the largest archery manufacturing company in the world. They not only sell volumes of bows; they sell a product of superior design and excellence in craftsmanship. The combination of quantity and quality is a rare blend seen in the business community today. But the commitment of the McPherson family to honor God in all they do has increased the favor of God on all they do.

Not all creative ideas have to come from a suspended piece of paper. As exciting as Matt's story is, the bigger picture is of a man and wife who have given themselves completely to God, for His glory. It is because God found them trustworthy that He entrusted ideas of great worth to them. Matt is the owner of at least 20 patents, with more pending. They have embraced the call to ministry through business. He was inducted into the Bowhunters Hall of Fame in 1998.

Before his breakthrough in the archery industry, Matt ran a body repair shop that shared space with another repair shop. One day he observed one of the other tenants deliberately damaging a vehicle, so he could collect more insurance. Matt addressed the situation; the other tenant's response to Matt was that no one was getting hurt, and that you had to be willing to compromise in that business to make a living. Matt told him he was wrong, and set out to prove that success can come without the loss of personal integrity. Today, as far as Matt knows, that man is still eking out a living while Matt is demonstrating the blessing that comes from honorable living—a wealth that has no sorrow.

The same excellence and creativity used for designing and manufacturing archery equipment is also used for making acoustic guitars. As a result of their innovation and quality, their master craftsmen make some of the finest guitars in the country. Many of the industry's top recording artists play the McPherson guitar. This is yet another testimony of the McPherson story of God's promised blessing. When Matt once asked God why he was chosen for a particular assignment, he discovered that while he wasn't God's first choice, he was the first willing. The assignment was challenging, but successful.

Today Matt and Sherry McPherson are living what God had promised many years ago. They are free to do their music ministry, travel, and support the Gospel around the world. They have also discovered the joy of bringing God-ideas to their sphere of influence. As a result, their business is ministry. Countless numbers of people are touched by their love and example in the business world through their integrity, creativity, and excellence.

ANSWERS FROM A HOMELESS SHELTER

One of the more unique expressions of innovation comes from a most unlikely place—a homeless shelter in Southern California. It is called Hope for Homeless Youth, and is pastored by Clayton Golliher, a member of the Harvest International Ministries network. Clayton and his group have tapped into God's creative nature, and have made that privilege a part of their discipleship training. As a result they already have 12 patents that have captured the attention of major toy makers and manufacturers around the country. The shelter sees these open doors for business as open doors for the ministry of the Gospel. Executives of major corporations have been amazed by their inventions, which have produced an openness to their message. To say they are shocked by *who God gives the ideas to is a great understatement.*

One of the toys already in production is their *anti-gravity hovercraft* flying machine. It is being m-ade in China and will most likely be sold nationwide through a TV marketing network. This *one-of-a-kind* toy has opened doors for ministry that has already resulted in conversions to Christ in that communist nation. It's remarkable; creativity turns the heads of those in big business, resulting in conversions to Jesus Christ!

One expert told them their idea for the hovercraft would be "aerodynamically impossible to fly." So they went to prayer, where God gave them a vision showing them how to make it, what materials to use, and how it would fly. It was up and flying within two days.

Besides the unique toys, they have over 50 "household type" inventions. They have amazing ideas that range from a *cure for diaper rash* to a device that dramatically *cuts a household's water consumption.*

They attribute their success to three things:

1. They believe that they live under an "open Heaven." Because of what Jesus did on the Cross they can be one with God. His creativity has been interwoven into them through Christ.

2. They believe they have dominion over this world: over the economy and the technologies of this earth.

3. They pray in the Spirit up to three hours a day. They believe that when they pray in tongues they tap into the Holy Spirit's creative nature.

Their amazing story is more than simply a bunch of Christians learning how to be creative. That story in itself would be worth telling. But this is a story of this nation's "throwaways" bringing solutions to everyday problems and challenges. It is a marvelous reflection of God's grace and one man's vision functioning outside the box of normal ministry expectations. Perhaps this is part of what the Lord had in mind when the prophet declared, "*I will make the lame a remnant, and the outcast a strong nation...*" (Micah 4:7).

A TRAVELER'S PRAYER

Not every creative expression has to do with inventions, or solving problems. Sometimes this characteristic is seen in the caring way we express the love of God to others. The previous three stories were all about the influence of the Kingdom on invention and design; this next story is about communication.

On a recent visit to Dallas, Texas, I returned to my room at the Embassy Suites Hotel following the evening meeting. Leaning against my pillow was a laminated card that one of the hotel staff left after cleaning my room. Thinking it was just another notice about a particular feature of the hotel, I started to lay it aside. Then I saw it was a prayer. Out of curiosity I began to read. I've never seen anything so simple, yet so profound, which actually has the potential to bring great impact to a person or even a city. It represents the responsibility of Kingdom-oriented people to be a contributor to society for their good. Once again we see that creative Kingdom influence can and must be demonstrated in all we do, big and small. It's called an *Ancient Prayer* – "The Stranger Within Our Gates."

Because this hotel is a human institution to serve people,
and not solely a money making organization,
we hope that God will grant you peace and rest
while you are under our roof.

May this room and hotel be your "second" home.
May those you love be near you in thoughts and dreams.
Even though we may not get to know you,
we hope that you will be comfortable and happy
as if you were in your own house.

May the business that brought you our way prosper.
May every call you make
and every message you receive
add to your joy.
When you leave, may your journey be safe.

We are all travelers. From "birth till death"
we travel between eternities.
May these days be pleasant for you,
profitable for society, helpful for those you meet,
and a joy to those who know and love you best.

It is amazing to me that something with that level of Kingdom principle would be left on a pillow in a hotel room...particularly a major hotel chain. This is especially noteworthy when you consider the *politically correct* conflict that exists in the minds of most CEO's. I honor the person who decided to take this risk by impacting lives with such a compassionate prayer of blessing. It not only functions as a powerful prayer, it gives an opportunity for people to adjust their thinking to Kingdom principles, while potentially gaining a sense of purpose for why they are on planet earth.

How and what we communicate has the potential to change the atmosphere, creating the context for people to be released to their destiny. Therefore our communication skills must come under the influence of the Holy Spirit. Done correctly, our words are able to release the presence of God into people's lives through the expressions of compassion and concern.

THERE'S MORE

To consistently bring these kinds of solutions to the forefront of society, we will have to learn how to access the realm of Heaven; for it is in Heaven where our answers lie. The spirit of revelation has been given to make this possible. That is the focus of the next chapter.

CHAPTER 7

The Spirit of Revelation

We thrive with the spirit of revelation,
but we perish without it.

People who see what is unseen have the advantage over everyone else who desire a place of significance.[1] They are the
ones who are able to *live from Heaven toward earth*. When we live
conscious of Heaven and eternity, it changes the way we live and radically increases our measure of impact on society. It's really quite
amazing that the ones who see Heaven most clearly have little desire
for this world, yet they are the ones who have the greatest impact on
the world around them.

Awareness of unseen things is a vital aspect of the Christian life.
In fact, we are instructed to, "*Set your mind on the things above, not
on the things that are on earth. For you have died and your life is hidden with Christ in God*" (Col. 3:2-3). The abundant life that Jesus
promised to His disciples is found in this unseen realm. The display
of His dominion through miracles and various supernatural expressions are all rooted in this heavenly world. We must access His world
to change this one.

The Impossible Assignment

Changing the course of world history is our assignment. Yet we have gone as far as we can with what we presently know.[2] We need signs to get where we want to go. Signs are realities that point to a greater reality—an exit sign is real, but it points to something greater—the exit.[3] We don't need signs when we travel on familiar roads. But, if we're going to go where we've never gone before, we'll need signs to get there. These *signs* will restore the *wonder*.

To go any further we need to hear from God anew. We must see the things that are before our faces day after day, yet are presently hidden from our eyes. The ever present need to see and hear has never been greater. The key to staying current with the shifting seasons of God is the spirit of revelation.

The apostle Paul understood this need as he prayed for the church at Ephesus. He asked the Father to give them the Spirit of wisdom and revelation (see Eph. 1:17). Many would consider the church in Ephesus to be the most significant church in the Bible. They were experiencing one of the greatest revivals in history; second perhaps only to Nineveh (see Jonah 3). There was a public confrontation with the occult, which resulted in satanic materials being destroyed by repentant citizens (see Acts 19:19). Some of the New Testament's most notable miracles also happened there.

It is also the only church to receive a letter from the apostle Paul in which he gave no word of correction. In their letter he unveiled what is arguably the Bible's greatest revelation of spiritual warfare, husband and wife relationships/the Bride of Christ and Jesus, the fivefold ministry, the nature and function of the church, are a few examples.

For this victorious body of believers he prayed, "*That the God of our Lord Jesus Christ, the Father of glory, may give to you the spirit of wisdom and revelation in the knowledge of Him*" (Eph. 1:17). What do you give to the one who has everything? Prayer for their eyes to open to see what is still unseen (revelation), and the insight to know what to do with it once they see it (wisdom).

A fundamental lesson for us in this historic fact is that even a church in revival, known for great teaching and citywide impact, needs more revelation. It is not automatic. To say, "The Spirit of God is welcome here, and free to do as He pleases" is not enough. Many of the things we need and long for must be prayed for specifically, and pursued relentlessly. Such is the case with the spirit of wisdom and revelation. Only when wisdom and revelation are passionately pursued do they take the place they deserve in the Christian life. These two elements become the safeguards that keep us from the peril of religion. The foremost apostle prayed this for the foremost church.

WHY DO WE NEED REVELATION?

What I know will help me. What I think I know will hurt me. It's the spirit of revelation that helps me know the difference.

The prophets warned us about what would happen to a people who did not increase in knowledge through revelation. All knowledge is useful, but can be general. But when God releases revelation, it releases knowledge that enables us to address specific issues at crucial moments. It often is the difference between life and death. It can be said that we thrive with revelation knowledge but perish without it.

> My people are **destroyed for lack of knowledge**. Because you have rejected knowledge, I also will reject you from being My priest. Since you have forgotten the law of your God, I also will forget your children (Hosea 4:6 NASB).

And,

> Therefore My people **go into exile for their lack of knowledge**; and their honorable men are famished, and their multitude is parched with thirst (Isaiah 5:13 NASB).

The Old Testament prophets Hosea and Isaiah understood the challenge and spoke to the issues we would be facing. In the two passages there were two calamities mentioned. *Destroyed* means to "cease; to be completely cut off." Without revelation we are completely cut off from the purposes of God on the earth. It is possible to be busy about the Lord's work, yet still separated from His purposes. *Go into exile* is very similar in its meaning as it can also be translated as "remove." The picture here is of one who suffers an "official expulsion from a home, country or area as a punishment." Here we are exiled from His purposes, as we are unfit to carry the weightiness of such a responsibility apart from the spirit of revelation working in our lives. It is costly to have access to *sight*, and not use it (see Luke 12:56).

Knowledge in this context is experiential knowledge. It is more than mere concepts or theories. The word knowledge here comes from the word used in Genesis describing the experience of intimacy – "*And Adam knew Eve; and she conceived and bare Cain*" (Gen. 4:1 KJV).

It is foolish to think, "Because we have the Bible, the full revelation of God has already been given. We don't need anymore." First of all, while the Bible is complete (no more books are to be added) it is a closed book without the help of the Holy Spirit. We must have revelation to see what is already written. Secondly, we know so little of what God wants us to understand from His Word. Jesus said as much. He couldn't teach His disciples all that was in His heart (see John 16:12). This is the knowledge that comes from the Spirit of God as He breathes upon the pages of Scripture. It leads to divine encounters; truth experienced is never forgotten.

Another passage to examine in this line of thought is:

"*Where there is no vision, the people perish*" (Proverbs 29:18 KJV).

The New King James Version says, "*Where there is no revelation, the people cast off restraint.*" That clarification is huge. Many have thought this passage was about goals and dreams. It's not! It's about the impact of the spirit of revelation upon a person's life, enabling them to joyfully restrain themselves from everything that works against the dream of God for us. As someone once said, *vision gives pain a purpose.*

THE ASSIGNMENT

Not all truth is equal. Truth is multidimensional—some things are true, and some things are truer. If you touched a leper in the Old Testament, you became unclean. A primary revelation of the Old Testament is the power of sin. In the New Testament you touch the leper and the leper becomes clean. A primary revelation of the New Testament is the power of God's love. Both statements are true (*sin is powerful* and *love is powerful*) but one is clearly superior.

The Holy Spirit has been given to lead us into all truth. But one of the things He is so clearly in charge of is taking us into the truths that the Father wants emphasized in a particular season. Peter understood this when he wrote:

> *For this reason I will not be negligent to remind you always of these things, though you know and are established in the **present truth*** (2 Peter 1:12).

Present truth implies *truth that is at the forefront of God's thinking.* It is a wise man who learns to recognize where the winds of Heaven are blowing. Life and ministry are so much easier when we involve ourselves in what God is already blessing.

GREEN LIGHT DISTRICT

Many believers live with the concept that God will lead them when it's time for them to do something. And so they wait, sometimes for an entire lifetime, without any significant impact on the world around them. Their philosophy—I have a red light until God gives me a green one. The green light never comes.

The apostle Paul lived in the *green light district* of the Gospel. He didn't need signs in the heavens to convince him to obey the Scriptures. When Jesus said, "Go!" that was enough. But He still needed the Holy Spirit to show him what was at the forefront of the Father's mind concerning missions.

He had a burden for Asia, and tried to go there and preach. The Holy Spirit stopped him, which also means He didn't lead him. He then tried to go to Bithynia, but again, the Holy Spirit said no. He then had a dream of a man pleading with him to come to Macedonia. He woke up concluding that this was the direction he was looking for, and went to Macedonia to preach the Gospel. It's a wonderful story of God's leading (see Acts 16:6-10). But it's easy to miss the point; Paul was trying to obey what was on the pages of Scripture because he lived carrying the commandment *to go into all the world!* (See Matt. 28:19.) The old adage comes into play here; it's easier to steer the car when it's moving than when it's standing still. Paul's commitment to the lifestyle of *going* put him in the place to hear the specific directions God had for him in that season. It was the Holy Spirit who was trying to keep him from going to certain places in wrong seasons.

THE PURPOSE OF REVELATION

Revelation is not poured out to make us smarter. Insight is a wonderful benefit of this encounter, but our intelligence is not God's primary concern. His focus in revelation is our *personal transformation*. Revelation leads to a God encounter, and that encounter forever changes us. The encounters can be stunning experiences, or the simple moments of being immersed in His peace; but they are markers along the journey of, *"Thy kingdom come...."* Without the encounter, revelation makes us proud. This was the nature of Paul's warning to the church at Corinth: *"Knowledge puffs up..."* (1 Cor. 8:1). The actual effect on our intelligence is according to the measure of transformation we've experienced. Revelation comes to *enlarge the playing field of our faith.* Insight without faith being released to have the truth realized through experience keeps truth unproven—only theory. It is the birthplace of religion. When God shows us that He wants people well, it is not to give us a theology on healing. It is so we will release our faith into the very area in which He's given us insight that we might experience the fruit of revelation—in this case, to heal people! *Revelation* means "to lift the veil" or "remove the cover." Revelation gives us access to the *realms of greater anointing available* to us to make that truth a personal experience and lifestyle. The greater the truth, the greater the anointing needed to demonstrate that truth to the world. Anointing must be pursued, not assumed (see 1 Cor. 14:1). The measure of anointing that we carry reveals the measure of revelation we actually live in.

The Heart that Receives

One of the more offensive concepts that Jesus taught and believed is that children are more ready to enter the Kingdom than grown-ups. Many of us have adjusted to the concept for the most part, but still struggle with certain applications. The following is a case in point:

> *At that time Jesus answered and said, "I thank You, Father, Lord of heaven and earth, that You have hidden these things from the wise and prudent and have revealed them to babes* (Matthew 11:25).

Can it be true that children are more open to revelation than adults? We tend to think that the weightier concepts are reserved for the mature. In part, that is true. But the really mature, from God's perspective, are those with a child's heart.

Many people ask me to pray for them to receive greater revelation from Scripture. While it's always an honor to bless someone with prayer, it is seldom understood how revelation comes, or to whom it comes. One of the greatest joys in life is hearing from God.

There is no downside. But there is a cost that comes with the impartation.

The following is a list of practical suggestions for those wanting to grow in revelation from God.

Become childlike. Simplicity and humility of heart helps qualify a person to hear from God, while the desire to be profound is a wasted desire. What many discover after years of teaching is that the word that is simple is often the most profound. *"At that time Jesus answered and said, "I thank You, Father, Lord of heaven and earth, that You have hidden these things from the wise and prudent and have revealed them to babes"* (Matt. 11:25).

Obey what you know. Jesus taught His followers, *"If anyone wills to do His will, he shall know concerning the doctrine, whether it is from God or whether I speak on My own authority"* (John 7:17). *"If anyone wills...he shall know"*—Clarity comes to the one willing to do the will of God. The willingness to obey attracts revelation, because God is the ultimate steward, investing His treasures into fertile ground—the surrendered heart.

Learn the biblical art of "meditation." *"I call to remembrance my song in the night; I will meditate within my heart, and my spirit makes diligent search"* (Ps. 77:6). Biblical meditation is a diligent search. Whereas religious cults teach people to empty their minds as the means of meditation, the Bible teaches us to fill our minds with God's Word. Meditation has a quiet heart and a "directed" mind. Mulling a word over in our heart, with a pursuit that springs from the inquisitive child's heart, is meditation.

Live in faith. Living by faith in my present assignment makes me ready for more. *"Whose minds the god of this age has blinded, who do not believe, lest the light of the gospel of the glory of Christ, who is the image of God, should shine on them"* (2 Cor. 4:4). Notice that the light of the Gospel comes to the person who believes. Revelation comes to the one expressing faith! Live with the understanding that God has already willed to give you His mysteries (see Matt. 13:11), and ask accordingly. Then thank Him in advance.

Acquire an understanding heart. This sort of heart has the foundations in place for something to be constructed upon it. These are the basic concepts of the King and His Kingdom. Proper foundations attract the builder (revelator) to come and add to those foundations. "*But knowledge is easy to one who has understanding*" (Prov. 14:6 NASB). God wisely stewards fresh insight to those who have the basic principles in place. When fresh insights come, the understanding heart has a "slot to put it in." It is not lost as seed spilled on the ground.

Give God your nights. I try to end each day with my heart's affection stirred up and directed to the Holy Spirit. What an amazing way to go to sleep. The Song of Solomon reveals this poetically, "*I sleep, but my heart is awake*" (Song of Sol. 5:2). God loves to visit us in the night and give us instruction that we would have a hard time receiving during the day (see Job 33:15-16). The desire to give God our night season flows naturally from the child's heart that knows revelation cannot be earned. Ask Him specifically to minister to you in the night through visions and dreams. Once you have a dream or vision, write it out, and ask Him for understanding.

Give away what you have already received. Never underestimate what hungry people can "pull" from you while you minister the Word. Being in a place of continual giving is a sure way of getting more. When we're in "over our heads" in a ministry situation, we find out what God has been putting into us during the night. He draws out of the deep places in our hearts things that are not yet a part of our conscious thought processes (see Prov. 20:5).

Become a friend of God. God shares His secrets with His friends. "*No longer do I call you servants, for a servant does not know what his master is doing; but I have called you friends, for all things that I heard from My Father I have made known to you*" (John 15:15). He makes all things known to His friends. Not only does He want to share all, He's invited us to ask anything of Him. But be accustomed to hearing more than you can share with others. Listen as He speaks, but speak only what He gives you freedom to speak about. Some things are revealed only because we're friends, and are not to be shared with others.

INHERITING THE FAMILY STORIES

One of the fun parts of growing up was hearing stories of my family. It didn't matter if it was Grandpa talking about the Northern Pike he caught in Minnesota, or it was my dad talking about his days playing football in high school, they were the stories I loved to hear. And it didn't matter that we may have heard them last week. I wanted to hear them again and again, hoping each time I might get more detail. They were worth repeating, and are a part of my inheritance.

In this light, Jesus made some alarming statements. He said, *"Truly, truly, I say to you, we speak of what we know and testify of what we have seen, and you do not accept our testimony. If I told you earthly things and you do not believe, how will you believe if I tell you heavenly things?"* (John 3:11-12 NASB).

"We" refers to the Father, the Son, and the Holy Spirit. It is NOT a reference to Jesus and His disciples or even Jesus and the angels. Jesus said what He heard His Father say. The Spirit of God was upon Him, and made it possible for Him to succeed in hearing and seeing His Father clearly. God has a testimony, and is trying to pass on His story to anyone who would listen. He repeats His cry later in this chapter, *"What He has seen and heard, of that He testifies; and no one receives His testimony"* (John 3:32 NASB). Because it's our responsibility to *"loose here what is loosed in heaven"* (Matt. 16:19), we need to have a revelation of Heaven along with the heart to hear His testimony. That is the benefit of *"being seated in heavenly places in Christ."* He desires to give us His testimony, but can't find anyone ready to hear it. He has spoken of earthy things (natural birth and the nature of wind; see John 3:1-8) and the people struggled—His desire is to speak to them of heavenly things, which have no earthly parallel.

HEAVY WORDS

Jesus couldn't teach His disciples all that was in His heart. He ached to give them more, but didn't because the weightiness of His words would crush them.

I have many more things to say to you, but you cannot bear them now (John 16:12 NASB).

Their "weight-carrying capacity" was insufficient for what Jesus had to say. When God speaks, He creates. The realities created from what Jesus would have liked to declare were far too significant for them. And the realms of glory released over their lives would require a strength and stability that they did not yet possess.

While it's true that God does not give His glory to another, we're not *another*—we are members of His Body. The ability to carry more has to do with both character and faith. Character enables us to receive glorious promises of destiny without taking the glory to ourselves. And greater faith responds to the declarations with the great courage needed for fulfillment.

The Holy Spirit was given to prepare them for revelation at a whole new level. He would take them where Jesus couldn't. Perhaps this is part of the reason Jesus said, "*It is to your advantage that I go….*" The indwelling Holy Spirit enables us to bear more of the revelation of Jesus than was possible for the original twelve disciples.

But when He, the Spirit of truth, comes, He will guide you into all the truth; for He will not speak on His own initiative, but whatever He hears, He will speak; and He will disclose to you what is to come. He will glorify Me, for He will take of Mine and will disclose it to you. All things that the Father has are Mine; therefore I said that He takes of Mine and will dis-close it to you (John 16:13-15 NASB).

The Holy Spirit is assigned to take us into *all truth*. The word *all* here is staggering, and should be. What makes this even more stunning is the realization that truth is to be experienced; the Holy Spirit is therefore leading us into experiencing *all truth*. He receives all of His instructions from the Father. It was the Holy Spirit upon Jesus that enabled Him to know what the Father was doing and saying. That *same gift* of the Spirit has been given to us for that *same purpose.*

One of the assignments of the Holy Spirit is to let us know *what is to come*. If you read commentaries and various reference materials, you'll notice most think the promise of *knowing what's coming* is all about us being aware of coming calamities. Theologians tend to focus on problems because few truly believe in the glorious church. Everyone from world leaders to musicians, to actors and business leaders, are telling us of the coming calamities. We don't need the Holy Spirit for that purpose when people without God can do it. Rather, we need Him to see the coming *glory*! The warnings of difficulties are necessary as they help us keep our priorities straight. But it's the Father's good pleasure to give us the mysteries of the Kingdom. And there's no pleasure in speaking of the death and destruction of the unrighteous (see Ezek. 33:11). It's still called the *good* news for a reason.

He goes on to say, *"He will glorify Me, for He will take of Mine and will disclose it to you."* A most touching thing takes place in this verse—Jesus inherits that which He previously gave up when He became a man and died in our place. It is also true that the Holy Spirit was given the task of not simply revealing all that Jesus possesses, but to actually "disclose" it to us. Disclose means to *declare*! There is an amazing transfer of resources taking place in this statement. Follow this; all belongs to the Father—the Father gives everything to the Son—the Son gives everything to us through the Holy

Spirit who transfers the resources of Heaven into our account through the declaration. This is astonishing! This is why hearing from God is so vital. He transfers Jesus' inheritance into our accounts every time He speaks. Every declared promise is a transfer of heavenly resources that enable us to fulfill the purpose of our commission.

DISCOVERING OUR INHERITANCE

One of the Holy Spirit's primary functions is to discover what lies in the depths of God's heart for us. He leads us into an understanding by experience to help us realize our inheritance.

> *For to us God revealed them through the Spirit; for the Spirit searches all things, even the depths of God. ...Now we have received, not the spirit of the world, but the Spirit who is from God, so that we may know the things freely given to us by God, which things we also speak, not in words taught by human wisdom, but in those taught by the Spirit, combining spiritual thoughts with spiritual words* (1 Corinthians 2:10, 12-13 NASB).

This inheritance is freely given to us; it is the Holy Spirit who brings us into that *land of promise* that we might correctly navigate our way through life realizing the height, depth, length, and width of God's extravagant love for us. He unveils what is ours.

He is also the one who makes the Scriptures come alive; it is the *living* Word. Learning to recognize His presence, His ways, and His language will help us to succeed in our impossible assignment. That is the focus of the next chapter.

ENDNOTES

1. Significance is a God-given desire. Living to be famous is its counterfeit.

2. Quote from Martin Scott.

3. Quote from Dick Joyce.

CHAPTER 8

Celebrating the Living Word

*It's difficult to get the same fruit
as the early church when we value a book they
didn't have more than the Holy Spirit they did have.*

God spoke and the worlds were made. His Word creates. The ability to hear God, especially from His Word, is a mandatory skill if we are to enter divine purpose and true creative expression. It's as necessary as breathing. A yielded heart is impressionable as it studies Scripture and receives God's impressions (fingerprints) easily. Within that sort of tender soil, the Lord plants the seeds of Kingdom perspective that grow into global transformation.

The insights and empowering nature of Scripture provide solutions applicable to every society and culture. The Bible is limitless in scope, timeless, and complete, containing answers to every dilemma of humanity. The study of Scriptures must take us beyond the historical setting, beyond language studies in the Hebrew and Greek, and at times beyond the context and intent of the human authors of Scripture. It's time to hear from God afresh—that His Word would once again become the living Word in our experience.

I believe the Bible to be the Word of God, inerrant, fully inspired by the Holy Spirit. It is without equal, not to be added to, nor subtracted from. Not only did God inspire the writers, He inspired those who selected which respective writings should be included to make up the full 66 books of the Bible. I do not believe there will be any new revelation that has the same authoritative weight as Scripture. It alone stands as judge of all other wisdom, be it the wisdom of man or an insight or book purported to be revealed directly from God or given by an angel. God is still speaking but everything we hear must be consistent with what He has spoken to us in His Word. In light of these burning convictions, there are standards and traditions instituted by the church for our protection that practically suck the life and impact out of God's living Word. Though not the original intent, it has been an unintended result.

Being unaware of His presence has cost us dearly, especially as we approach Scripture. King David, who authored and sang songs of His love for God's Word, "set" the Lord before himself daily. He purposed to be regularly conscious of God's nearness and lived from that mind-set. The sanctified imagination is a tool in God's hand that enables us to tap into true reality. My approach is this; since I can't imagine a place where He isn't, I might as well imagine Him with me. This is not vain imagination. Rather, it's vain to imagine otherwise.

LIVING BY PRINCIPLE OR PRESENCE

There is a style of Scripture reading that is mainly concerned with finding and applying principles rather than enjoying His presence. This is good but limited. Kingdom principles are real and powerful. They can be taught to anyone. When they are applied to life, they bring forth fruit for the King. Even unbelievers will experience blessing when they live by His principles. My friend was having financial problems. He confided in a neighbor, who also happened to be a pastor, and the minister told him that his problems could be due to the fact that he wasn't honoring God with the tithe—10 percent of his income. He then challenged my friend to test God by tithing to see if his counsel was accurate. When my friend tithed in response to the challenge, blessing starting pouring into his life. He ended up giving his life to Christ because he saw and tasted God's love. But notice the Kingdom principle functioned even before his conversion. Finding and applying principles is something even an unbeliever can do.

I am not knocking the principles. The transformation of cities and nations depends on the receptivity of Kingdom principles. However, this is not the core of the Christian's experience with the Bible. Rather, more often than not, we should read to have a God-encounter.

LEARNING TO HEAR GOD

I began learning to recognize God's voice through the study of Scripture. During one season of my life I spent considerable time in the Book of Ephesians. When I read, *"and to know the love of Christ which surpasses knowledge, that you may be filled up to all the fullness of God"* (Eph. 3:19), the Holy Spirit spoke to me. He told me that it meant that I could know by experience what would be beyond the reach of comprehension. Later I was able to do a word study and found that this was exactly the meaning of the verse in the original language.

Often I would come to the Bible with a need and God would address it clearly from His Word, again and again. There were times when He spoke so clearly from a verse, yet I knew that what was ministering to me wasn't what the writer originally intended. But it was a *living word*, a sword, ministering to the very need of my heart. It wasn't until years later that I learned that God didn't speak that way anymore.

I'm thankful I learned to hear God through the Scriptures before I found out what the rules were. It's like being told there are no miracles today. That laughable statement might have gotten my attention many years ago, but it's way too late now. I've seen thousands.

THE ERROR THAT BREEDS ERRORS

To value the Scriptures above the Holy Spirit is idolatry. It is not Father, Son, and Holy Bible; it's the Holy Spirit. The Bible reveals God, but is itself not God. It does not contain Him. God is bigger than His book. We are reliant on the Holy Spirit to reveal what is contained on the pages of Scripture, because without Him it is a closed book. Such dependency on the Holy Spirit must be more than a token prayer asking for guidance before a Bible study. It is a relationship with the third person of the Trinity that is continuous, ongoing, and affects every single aspect of life. He is the wind that blows in uncertain directions, from unknown places (see John 3:8). He is the power of Heaven, and cannot be controlled, but must be yielded to. He eagerly reveals His mysteries to all who are hungry—truly hungry. He is so valued in Heaven that He comes with a warning. The Father and Son can be sinned against, but sinning against the Holy Spirit has unforgivable eternal consequences.

The Holy Spirit is de-emphasized and almost removed from many Christian's daily approach to life and the Word. The fear of becoming like some mindless fanatic has kept many a Christian from interacting with their greatest treasure in this life—the Holy Spirit. We are heirs of God, and the Holy Spirit is the down payment of our inheritance (see Eph. 1:13-14). Some teach that we shouldn't talk much about the Spirit as the Holy Spirit doesn't speak of Himself. However, both the Father and Son have a lot to say about Him. It is wise to listen to them. God is to be praised, adored, boasted in, and interacted with—and the Holy Spirit is God.

The approach of many believers to Scripture is inconsistent with the Spirit who inspired those sacred writings. Much of what we have a heart to accomplish cannot be done without reexamining our relationship with God through His Word. We have gone as far as we can go with what we presently know. Not only are we in need of the Spirit of God to teach us, we are in need of a different view of the Bible.

The God who speaks through circumstances and unusual coincidences wants to talk to us again through the pages of His Word, even when it appears to be taken out of context or is not exactly in line with what appears to be the author's original intent.

THE LIVING WORD

The Word of God is living and active. It contains divine energy, always moving and accomplishing His purposes. It is the surgeon's knife that cuts in order to heal. It is balm that brings comfort and healing. But the point I wish to stress is that it is multidimensional and unfolding in nature. For example, when Isaiah spoke a word, it applied to the people he spoke to—his contemporaries. Yet because it is alive, much of what he said then has its ultimate fulfillment in another day and time. Living words do that.

God said we were to choose whom we would serve, yet Jesus said He chose us; we didn't choose Him. We are predestined from before the foundation of the world, yet are told that *whosoever will* may come. Jesus said we had to sell all to follow Him, yet He instructs the wealthy to be rich in good works.[1] The Holy Spirit knows what truth to breath on according to the particular season of our life.

A classic conflict to the Western rational mind is found in Proverbs' instruction on how to treat a fool. It says, "*Do not answer a fool according to his folly, or you will also be like him.*" The very next verse says, "*Answer a fool as his folly deserves, that he not be wise in his own eyes*" (Prov. 26:4-5). One verse says *not to answer a fool,* and it tells you why. Then it says to *answer a fool,* also giving us the reasons why. This is not a contradiction to the Hebrew mind-set, which understands that truth is often held in the tension of two conflicting ideas.

The mind-set that wants static, unmovable, tidy boundaries, and interpretations gets offended over the lines of reason and expectation that seem be in flux. Herein lies our great challenge—can we hear what He is saying now, for now? And can we accept that He may speak differently to each of us?

ALL TRUTH IS NOT CREATED EQUAL

Truth is multidimensional. Some truths are superior to others. Lesser truths are often the foundation of greater truths. "I no longer call you servants, but friends." Friendship with God is built on the foundation of first being a servant. Truth is progressive in nature— line upon line, precept on precept.

For example, the primary message of the Old Testament is to reveal the power of sin. For that reason when a person touched a leper, they became unclean. Sin is overpowering. Flee from it! The primary message of the New Testament is the power of God's love. So when Jesus touched a leper, the leper became clean. "Love covers a multitude of sin." Both messages are true. One is greater. Love is overpowering!

Much division takes place in the church when people are devoted to different levels of truth. We tend to prefer static rules and boundaries, not things that flex and change. This desire for static rules is our basic preference for the law. Preset boundaries are what keep us *obedience focused* instead of *relationship focused*. One is set on memorized rules and regulations. The other is entirely set on His voice and presence and the rules and regulations sit at a different level. When the woman caught in adultery was brought before Jesus, He decided to enforce His own rules and law in a way contrary to what the law demanded. And Jesus only did what He saw the Father doing. Obedience will always be important for us. But obedience out of love looks a lot different than obedience because of rules. Israel discovered they couldn't do it, and neither can we.

To say the Scripture changes is an uncomfortable concept. It doesn't change in the sense that it passes away or contradicts itself, but it does change in the same way a wineskin expands to reflect the ever-increasing move of the Spirit of God. In Deuteronomy 23:1 the Lord commands that an emasculated man "*shall not enter the assembly of the Lord.*" Yet in Isaiah 53:3-5, the eunuch who holds fast to the covenant will be given an everlasting name which will not be cut off. Finally, in Acts 8, Phillip converts a eunuch who becomes the very first evangelist to Ethiopia. Peter called this sort of movement "present truth."

OUT OF CONTEXT

In studying the Old Testament prophecies quoted in the New Testament, it doesn't take long to realize that Jesus and other writers of Scripture took many Old Testament passages out of context to prove their point. The common thought today is that the Holy Spirit worked that way for the Scriptures to be written, but it is unacceptable to do this today because the canon[2] is complete. How could it be wrong to use the same principles used to write the Scriptures to interpret the Scriptures? That *rule* is designed to keep us from creating doctrine by experience and contradicting orthodox Christianity. While the reason is noble, the rule is not biblical. It keeps us from some of the fruitfulness that has been assigned to the church of this hour.

The rule was written because we are unfamiliar with the presence and voice of Holy Spirit. The problem is not our tendency to incorrectly interpret Scripture; it's that after 2,000 years with the Holy Spirit being on the earth and in us, we still don't know Him! The rule is not the answer. Repentance for ignoring the third person of the Trinity is the beginning of the much-needed solution. That alone can take us into realms in God that have previously been thought impossible for an entire generation to experience.

How is it possible to set a rule of Bible interpretation that the Holy Spirit Himself did not follow in inspiring the Bible? And to say that it is no longer allowed because the canon is complete has little merit as the Holy Spirit is with us, and He knows what He meant when He wrote it. This is potentially dangerous because of the bent of some toward creating unholy and/or inaccurate doctrine, but it does not justify removing a necessary tool of the Spirit that He uses to speak to His people. There is danger, but there is also great treasure. This is the necessary tension.

A NEW NON-BURSTING WINESKIN

Doctrine must be a wineskin kept elastic by the oil of the Spirit. If it is rigid and unmoving, it will not yield to God's habit of opening up more of His Word to us. God loves to add to our knowledge things we think we already understand. Too much rigidity bursts our doctrinal wineskins under the weight of ongoing revelation. The end result is the church becomes irrelevant and powerless to the world around them.

It is easy to prefer a particular theological slant, build a monument around it, and become deaf or adversarial to its important counterpoint. For example, I am much more Armenian in background than I am Calvinist. Yet some of my dearest friends are Calvinists. I love to hear the Holy Spirit work through them, because there is freshness to what they teach. I become convinced of God's sovereignty and leave that meeting with a conviction that "God chose me, I didn't choose Him!" Conversely, when I sit in a meeting where the opposite point is stressed, I also leave with conviction—that of freewill, the power of our choice, my responsibility as a delegated one on this planet, and that the outcome of His purposes depends upon the faithfulness of God's people. Which is true? Both are.

The Holy Spirit has to be free to speak to us about the things that are on His heart; especially to those things we have a natural resistance. We must be open to truth when it has a biblical basis and is accompanied by the breath of God making it come alive for a specific purpose. The error is building a theological monument around a particular point of view that conveniently excludes certain portions of Scripture to help us feel secure in a doctrinal bent.

I am also concerned with our tendency to gather around doctrines instead of around spiritual fathers. The former builds denominations, while the latter creates movements. Even our most valued doctrines can be expanded under the inspiration of the Holy Spirit. Usually, it's not the expansion that we have the most difficulty with. It is when He begins to speak about what is, at first glace, a contradiction to what we have learned. The desire for rigid doctrine is in direct proportion to our inability to actually hear His voice. It's essential to be able to recognize His voice so we can embrace His revelation, even when it contradicts our traditional upbringing.

God is big enough to feed me from a particular verse everyday for the rest of my life. The Word of God is infinitely deep. I must come to that which I understand with a childlike heart because what I know can keep me from what I need to know if I don't remain a novice. Becoming an expert in any area of Scripture is the very thing that often closes us off from learning the new things that God is opening up in His Word.[3] Again, it's the childlike heart that attracts revelation from God (see Matt. 11:25).

JESUS CHRIST, THE ULTIMATE REVELATION

The one revelation that is about to change everything is the revelation of Jesus Christ. Paul declared as much when he said that there was something we would come to know by revelation (see Eph. 1:17) that would bring us into the fullness of Christ, saying *"until we all attain to the unity of the faith, and of **the knowledge of the Son of God**, to a mature man, to the measure of the stature which belongs to **the fullness of Christ**"* (Eph 4:13). Notice that coming into maturity is the result of gaining the *knowledge of the Son of God*. This revelation will completely change the church as we know it today, *because as we see Him we become like Him*. This will enable us to accurately represent Jesus.

Jesus Christ is perfect theology. He is the *"…exact representation of His nature…"* (Heb. 1:3 NASB), the ultimate portrayal of the Father. Questions that exist about God's nature in the Old Testament were clarified in the New Testament. When I teach about God's absolute desire and provision to heal, I am asked, "what about

Job?" I respond, "I'm not a disciple of Job, I'm a disciple of Jesus." Job's life helped create the awareness for the need of a savior. Job is the question. Jesus is the answer. If our study of Job (and other Old Testament issues) doesn't lead us to Jesus as the answer, it reveals we never really understood the question. The types and symbols of the Old Testament do not override the clear manifestation of God through Jesus in the New Testament. Any understanding we have about the nature of God that can't be seen in the person of Jesus, must be questioned.

How many people came to Jesus for a miracle and left disappointed? None! He was 100 percent successful as a man dependant on God. Jesus also messed up every funeral He attended, including His own. When the disciples asked Him about their failed attempt to bring deliverance to a child, He gave them instructions on how to get their breakthrough. He said it would come through *prayer and fasting* (Mark 9:29). It's time to respond to His counsel and discover for ourselves how to get the breakthrough that appears to be so elusive. He manifested the will of God. And we must not change it to fit our experience. It is time to manifest the will of God again.

THE REALITY AND VALUE OF DANGER

It is obvious and easy to assert that those who try to hear God from the pages of Scripture will not always hear clearly. Some of us will make huge mistakes and claim to have heard from God when it wasn't Him at all. Yet, to succeed, one must be willing to fail.

Early in our first pastorate, one of the elders of the church announced that he and his wife were expecting a child. It would be their third, and quite a surprise. We all rejoiced with them because of this wonderful news. As the time of delivery drew near, the doctor gave them the worst news possible—the baby in her womb was dead. When they came to us with the news, we all rallied together in prayer. It seemed that everywhere I looked in the Bible I found verses on resurrection. So, based on this, as a church we declared that this baby was not dead but alive. We prophesied the best we knew how. When the day of delivery came, the baby was in fact born dead. There was great mourning; first because of their heartbreak and loss, and second, because we didn't actually hear from God and missed it with all of our prophetic pronouncements. We met as a church family to review the tragedy and our mistakes. And as carefully as I knew how, I addressed where we missed God and tried to encourage everyone to press on in spite of our disappointment and loss.

We have since had at least two babies whom the doctors pronounced dead in the womb, be resurrected and born alive and well. (One mother had been examined by five different medical professionals, all with the same conclusion—the baby is dead. Each of them gave her the warning that she would die if they were not allowed to remove the child. Jesus, in His mercy, raised the baby to life in her womb.) The area of our greatest risk, though we have previously failed, can become our greatest area of authority, if we won't give up.

Early in the 20th century there was a gathering of believers who had tasted the power of God and were hungering for more. Many went to foreign countries to become missionaries but didn't bother learning the language because they knew that God would give it to them because they spoke in tongues. Great disappointment soon followed when they arrived and were unable to speak the national language. *"Hope deferred makes the heart sick,"* is a verse that was never truer than in those years of well-intentioned missionary efforts. Yet today there are many who have had such a miracle—receiving the miraculous ability to speak in a foreign language without training. I know of a couple of people who speak over 10 completely different languages, many of which they received when they went into the new area to evangelize. While it's not an excuse to neglect training, it is a reward for the previous generations' efforts, even though they thought they had failed.

Many years ago a notable leader in the Body of Christ told me he had consciously gotten rid of the prophetic ministry in his church. He felt there was too much danger and too many potential problems. I respected him too much to voice my disagreement, but I quietly got excited in my heart because in the natural, counterfeiters don't make fake pennies; it's not worth the effort. I knew that if the enemy worked that hard to create a counterfeit, the original must have great value. Only things of eternal consequence are worth the devil's attention. For that reason I get encouraged when I see areas of danger, like the prophetic.

My solution is to find people of like mind to work with, realize the danger involved in our common pursuit, and stay humble and accountable in our pursuit of the authentic.

THE APPROPRIATE RESPONSE TO DANGER

Often times the charismatic or Pentecostal groups are blamed for having poor theological foundations. Granted, the hunger for more takes some people "over the line." While this has been the cause of some of the mistakes in church history, it's certainly not the reason for most of them nor the most serious of them.

The most dangerous heresies are not usually from a zealous desire to hear and obey the rhema word of the Lord. Most often these tragedies involve a demonic (angel of light) visitation, either real or imagined, and the subsequent elevation of that so-called revelation to the authority of the Bible. However, it's a fact that many times throughout history there have been those who are wrongly inspired over a verse or a phrase in Scripture. The result has been the creation of wrong or poor doctrine. The need to be different and original has sponsored a lot of bad theology.

For instance, last century a gentleman was reading the account of the Mount Transfiguration experience. After Moses and Elijah disappeared, it says the disciples then saw "Jesus only" (see Matt.17:8). It seemed to him to be the rhema revelation that the church had been missing for all these years. There was no Trinity—Father, Son, and Holy Spirit. There was *only Jesus*. The Father and Holy Spirit were essentially Jesus in different forms. And so, another heresy was born.

The rules mentioned earlier were created, I'm sure, to protect us from such mistakes. But sometimes the rules that keep us from error also keep us from our destiny. I believe this to be one of those times. The appropriate response to dangerous, and intrinsically important ideas is to stay low, stay hungry, take risks, and keep accountable.

But the answer for many has been to take a more analytical approach to the Christian life, one that is stable in doctrine and disciplines but lives without personal experience, denies the opportunity for risk, and resists emotional expression and passion. Christianity was never to be known by its disciplines. It's to be known by its passion; and those without passion are in far more danger than they know. Demons are attracted to religiously sanitized environments where there is no power.

Furthermore, the focus of many denominations within the church upon proper theological foundations as the center of faith has not led them into an encounter with God that demonstrates the life, power, and glory of Christ. Jesus warned the Pharisees saying, *"You are mistaken, not understanding the Scriptures nor the power of God"* (Matt. 22:29). Both the Scriptures and the power of God are essential! There is no justification for lack in either area. The stream of theological accuracy and the stream of experiential Christianity will merge as we learn to give honor to one another in our pursuit of a full demonstration of the Gospel.

MEDITATION: THE THINKER'S WAY TO A NEW WINESKIN

Biblical meditation is a completely different animal than what is encouraged in the New Age culture. Theirs is a counterfeit because it encourages us to empty our minds, making them vulnerable to any *angel of light* to enter, and eventually control. Unfortunately, there are many evil spirits looking for a vacancy. True meditation feasts on God's Word. That absolute foundation for thought sets a course of direction that is sure to take one on the journey of a lifetime. It is interaction with the Holy Spirit. It's a good start for obtaining the new wineskin of thought addressed in Scripture, by giving time for the seed to germinate in a person's heart. "*Tremble, and do not sin. Meditate in your heart upon your bed, and be still*" (Ps. 4:4 NASB).

THE FRUITFULNESS OF MEDITATION

There is a very strange story in Genesis about Jacob and his deceitful father-in-law, Laban. He had worked for Laban, for what seemed like forever, and had been cheated over and over again. He wanted to break away from this costly relationship and establish his own home for his growing family. Jacob made a deal with Laban for a portion of the flocks to be given to him for his years of service. It would enable him to leave with something to start *life on his own.* They agreed that he would take all the spotted and speckled sheep and goats as his wages. Laban agreed to the terms knowing that spotted and speckled animals were an aberration. Genesis 30:37-39 (NASB) speaks of Jacob's cunning plan in this way:

> *Then Jacob took fresh rods of poplar and almond and plane trees, and peeled white stripes in them, exposing the white which was in the rods. He set the rods which he had peeled in front of the flocks in the gutters, even in the watering troughs, where the flocks came to drink; and they mated when they came to drink. So the flocks mated by the rods, and the flocks brought forth striped, speckled, and spotted.*

As the animals came to drink, they would see spotted and speckled rods in the ground near their watering hole, which was also their breeding ground. As they came to the water and bred, they did so while looking upon the spotted rods. The result was that they reproduced spotted and speckled offspring. And it was all because of what they saw when they came to the water.

More than once the Word of God is referred to as water. It cleanses us from the impurities of life in much the same way as the laver was used to purify the priests of the Old Testament before going into the presence of the Lord. The blood deals with sin, but it's water that addresses impurity (see Eph. 5:26). It's not an accident that the laver of water was made from the mirrors of the women, as the Bible tells us that the Word of God is like a mirror (see 1 Cor. 13:12; 2 Cor. 3:18; James 1:23).

I don't believe it to be a stretch in the intention of God to derive the following lesson from Jacob's story: when we come to God's Word, we will reproduce what we see. Even more interesting is this, which has become my personal experience—whatever my heart is set upon when I come to the Bible, will determine much of what I see in the Bible. That can be good or bad, depending on whether or not I have "*watched over my heart with all diligence*" (Prov. 4:23). Those with evil in their hearts can find the confirmation they are looking for through the misreading of Scripture. The problem is not the method or approach to the Bible; it is whether or not we are willing to stay humble, honest, and hungry before the Lord. Our desperation for truth makes us available for things that others seem to continually miss. Keeping a pure heart makes the journey to God's Word a journey where nothing is impossible.

If I come to God's Word with evangelism on my mind, it seems that evangelism is on every page of my Bible. All the stories reaffirm my understanding of God's heart for people, but open up new Scriptures that I never previously considered to be evangelistic. The same is true of finances. If I come to God's Word with money on my mind, it appears that the whole Bible teaches about stewardship. This principle is true of most any subject you could mention. What you carry to this watering hole will determine much of what you see and reproduce.

God desires for us to bring forth His solutions for the difficulties and traumas of life on this planet. When we carry our concerns before the Lord, which come from our place of influence and authority on this earth, He begins to open up His mysteries that are concealed in His Word. For example, if there's a conflict on the job between two friends, God will give you specific insight through His Word about how to bring peace. If there is a need to expand your business, but you're not sure about how or when, He will speak from the pages of His Word. It is living, immediately applicable, and unlimited in its scope and power.

His Word comes to life. He breathes on the pages of His book, and something happens in our hearts. It comes to life! In the end it comes down to this: we will reproduce what we see as we come to the water of His Word.

LEARNING TO SPEAK

As we study God's Word, the heart of God is revealed. All that He has declared will come to pass. His Word will not return without bearing the fruit that He intended (see Isa. 55:11). We have the privilege of saying what the Father is saying, and thereby learning how to shape our world through biblical declarations. That is the subject of the next chapter.

ENDNOTES

1. Jesus did that with the disciples. First they left all to follow: Matthew 19:29. Then He instructed them what to do with their money, and to make sure they owned a sword: Luke 22:36. God did the same with Israel; during their time in the wilderness they had to learn to trust Him for everything. Having no land of their own was their training ground to learn how to possess the Promised Land once they entered it.

2. The complete set of sacred writings forming the Bible, made up of 66 books.

3. When God reveals truth to us, it is always built on the foundation of previously revealed truth. The former is not discarded. It is what the fresh word is built upon.

CHAPTER 9

Redesigning Our World

*The Holy Spirit is imprisoned
in the bodies of unbelieving believers.*

In Chapter 1 we glanced at Adam's role in naming the animals. He was given the unique responsibility of co-laboring with God in designing the nature of the world he was going to live in. Is it possible we have been restored to that level of authority once again? Would the blood of Jesus do anything less? We have been given this amazing tool to fulfill our stewardship role; "*Death and life are in the power of the tongue...*" (Prov. 18:21 NASB). With our speech we design and alter our environment. Realities are created that didn't exist a moment earlier through simple proclamations. With this tool we can build up or tear down, edify or discourage, give life or destroy it. The declared word has the capacity to resource earth with Heaven's resources. As reformers we must first pay attention to what we say, realizing that we are actually building the world we have to live in. We have the ability to speak *from* God, revealing His world and His ways. As Bishop Joseph Garlington says, "*nothing happens in the Kingdom until something is said.*"

Jesus describes one of the primary roles of the Holy Spirit in this way; *"He will take of what is mine and declare it to you"* (John 16:14). He says this after revealing that all things belong to Him. Jesus is telling us how His inheritance (all things) would be transferred to our account. It would be done through the declaration. Every time God speaks to us, there is a transfer of heavenly resource from His account into ours. Hearing God is essential to the release and the discovery of the vastness of our inheritance in Christ. It is beyond comprehension. It is *all things* (1 Cor. 3:21).

The transfer of "all things," our inheritance, begs this question, "Why would God give us all things?" Because *all things* will be necessary for us to fulfill the commission that God has given us. Our assignment from God will require the use of "all things" to be under our supervision to accomplish His purposes on earth.

TOOL TIME

One of the essential tools necessary to redefine the nature of the world around us is the gift of *encouragement*. This profound instrument has all of Heaven's attention. When angels perceive its use, they know their assignment has been released. It is more than a natural use of words to make someone feel good about themselves or their circumstances; it is supernatural in nature and partners with Heaven to bring forth Heaven's response.

In the same way the Holy Spirit transfers our inheritance to us through the declaration, so we release heavenly realms through our speech. In God's economy, without declaration there is no creation (see Ps. 33:6). Deliberate declarations in line with the covenantal promises of God are essential for the transformation of the kingdoms of this world.

THE SET TIME OF FAVOR HAS COME

"And Jesus kept increasing in wisdom and stature, and in favor with God and men" (Luke 2:52 NASB). I understand why Jesus

needed to increase in favor with man, as it would give Him access and influence within society in ways He wouldn't have without favor. But how is it that the Son of God, who is perfect in every way, needs to increase in favor with God? I don't have an answer. But I do know this—if Jesus needed more favor from God to complete His assignment, how much more of an increase do I need!

As with most everything related to the Kingdom of God, we receive increase through generously giving away what we have. It is no different with favor—grace. *"Let no unwholesome word proceed from your mouth, but only such a word as is good for edification according to the need of the moment, so that it will give grace to those who hear"* (Eph. 4:29 NASB). In this passage we find that speaking words of edification brings grace into the life of the person we are speaking to. Grace is the favor of God; a highly valued heavenly commodity. This is a significant tool because it brings transformation through words of encouragement by attracting the favor of God to the one we choose to serve.

I have a prophet friend who has told me that if I want him to go to particular church, just tell him and he will go. The favor I have in the eyes of this wonderful man is transferable. He has given me the liberty to choose a place, and because of the favor I have in his eyes, he will give that favor to a church he doesn't even know. In a similar fashion we get to choose who to encourage, realizing that God will extend to them the favor we have received from Him. It is an issue of stewardship. If we question whether believers have actually been given such a role of eternal consequences, I remind you that Jesus said, *"If you forgive the sins of any, their sins have been forgiven them"* (John 20:23 NASB).

A CULTURE OF HONOR

Encouragement is the initial tool used to create what we call a *culture of honor*. We use honor to train believers to step into their destiny, to strengthen our community in righteousness, and even for evangelism. We have honored those in the various facets of our community with amazing results. The average unbeliever is not accustomed to Christians having something nice to say about them. Christianity is known more for what we don't like than for what we do like. In spite of our shortcomings, we have been given this wonderful gift to distinguish us from the rest—the grace to encourage. When we encourage, it is more than a *feel-good moment*; it actually releases the favor of God.

The truth that encouragement releases the supernatural activities of God into the environment, is a big issue in the Kingdom. In Isaiah 35:4, the people of God are told to minister to others with these words, *"Be strong, do not fear! Behold, your God will come with vengeance, with the recompense of God; He will come and save you."* That is encouragement founded upon the covenantal provision and promise of God. It is taking what is available by promise and declaring it into reality in a person's life. The angelic hosts recognize their assignment through the words spoken to insure they come to pass (see Ps. 103:20). The amazing response from Heaven is noteworthy: *"Then the eyes of the blind shall be opened, and the ears of the deaf shall be unstopped. Then the lame shall leap like a deer, and the tongue of the dumb sing..."* (Isa. 35:5-6). Impossibilities yield in the supernatural atmosphere of encouragement.

This atmosphere of honor creates a health from which we serve those around us with life. Instead of becoming the victim of our circumstances, our circumstances become our victims, bringing them under a covenantal purpose (see Rom. 8:28). We become the answer to the heartfelt cry of society.

LIVING INSIDE OUT

Contained in the realm of the Kingdom of God are all the answers to life's problems. It doesn't matter if it's the crisis with the ozone layer, frustration in dealing with contentious neighbors, or a problem with a failing marriage or business; the realm of the King's dominion has the answer. That realm of dominion is the realm of the Holy Spirit manifesting the lordship is Jesus Christ, which is first realized in our hearts.

Jesus taught us that, "...*the kingdom of God is within you*" (Luke 17:21). All the Kingdom issues are heart issues. Properly dealing with attitudes, ambitions, and agendas is key to enjoying the reign of God displayed in our lives. Our relationship with the Holy Spirit is foundational to the breakthroughs that we all want to see.

"*To you it has been granted to know the mysteries of the kingdom...*" (Luke 8:10 NASB). The secrets of God are our inheritance. We have access to this reality for the sake of those around us. The wonderful things that are to become manifest to the world are to flow from us. God intended that His expression to the world spring from *within* His people.

Israel was called upon to manifest the reign of God in their departure from Egypt and their entrance into the Promised Land. Normally this journey should have only lasted a couple of weeks at most, yet it took Israel 40 years. They *wandered* through the wilderness for 40 years. In reality, they were only doing on the outside what they were experiencing on the inside. "*Therefore I was angry with this generation, and said, 'They always go astray in their hearts, and they did not know my ways'; as I swore in my wrath, 'they shall not enter my rest'*" (Heb. 3:10-11 NASB). The phrase *go astray* means "to wander." They wandered in their hearts first. What was going on inside of them defined and shaped the world around them. In other words, their internal realities became their external realities. The lesson is simple: What is going on inside of us affects what goes on around us. This principle affects health, relationships, success in our occupation, and our gifts and ministries. All things flow from the heart. Solomon realized this and taught:

> *Watch over the heart with all diligence, for from it flows the issues of life* (Proverbs 4:23).

Stewardship of our heart is one of life's primary responsibilities. Successfully doing this guarantees success in other areas of life. When attitudes are properly guarded, godly conduct is insured. Careless attitudes give place to wrong thinking; and it's wrong thinking that gives way to sinful actions.[1]

PEACE ON EARTH

In Mark chapter 4 Jesus was in a life-threatening storm with the disciples. To their surprise, He was asleep. I've heard people say He slept because He was exhausted. I'd like to suggest that He slept because the world He was living in had no storms. Jesus was demonstrating what it was like to be *seated in heavenly places.* It is the exact application of what He meant when He said, that, "*...He who came down from Heaven, that is the Son of Man who is in heaven*" (John 3:13), even though He was clearly standing right in front of them on planet Earth.

They woke Him and said, "don't you care we are perishing?" which is an astounding question to ask the Savior of the world. He responded by speaking "peace" over the storm and the storm ended. The peace that enabled Him to rest in the middle of a conflict became the very substance He released that stilled the storm. In other words, His internal reality became His external reality. If it's in you, and it's genuine, it can be released through you. We have authority over any storm we can sleep in, as we can only give away what we've received.

DIVINE HEALTH AND PROSPERITY

This principle of the Kingdom affects all we are and do. It seems to be the heart behind "*Beloved, I pray that you may prosper in all things and be in health, just as your soul prospers*" (3 John 2). Once again we note that what is ruling on the inside of us affects the outside. Health in my emotions, mind, and will affects my physical well-being. It is also important to note that a prosperous soul attracts the blessing of the Lord materially and financially.[2] This is the nature of life. The reality of the heart helps to define the nature of the world around us.

ON EARTH, AS IT IS AT HOME

A stumbling block for many children raised in Christian homes is the fact that Mom and Dad act differently in church than they do at home. Sometimes it's an issue of out-and-out hypocrisy. But most of the time it is well-meaning believers who never learn to watch over their hearts. When anxiety and unrest rule over a person's heart, they automatically create that atmosphere in their home. The joy that is sung about in the corporate gathering is foreign where it's needed most—in the home.

This is actually the source of much burnout for Christians. There is a pressure to produce on the outside what doesn't exist on the inside. It manifests in a works-oriented Gospel that tries to obtain favor through labor rather than working from the place of favor.

Sometimes we focus on merely changing our words knowing that they carry creative force. Still it's out of the heart that the mouth speaks. Changing the external without dealing with the heart is the way of religion. The push for miracles is the same. Trying to obtain a measure of Kingdom expression on the outside that is not manifest on the inside is the sign that the cruel taskmaster of religion is present. In the command to do the miraculous we find the key, "*Freely you have received, freely give*" (Matt. 10:8). We can give away *kingdom* in the measure we experience the *King's dominion* within us. What reigns on the inside rains on the outside. As it was with Peter's shadow, whatever overshadows me will be released through my shadow (see Acts 5:15). The heart is capable of all sorts of evil as well as all sorts of significant spiritual breakthrough. Stewardship of the heart is what determines what is produced there.

PARTNERS WITH THE CREATOR

The soul that is bound by worry, jealousy, anger, resentment, and the like, is incapable of creativity on a consistent basis. It's impossible to thrive in that divine privilege because we are functioning separately from our design. Full potential is only found by carrying what God gave us to carry—"*my burden is light*" (Matt. 11:30). It is common knowledge that when a person's mind is not encumbered with these things, they are free for creative expression. Picture it like this—if I have an automobile with an eight-cylinder engine, I need all eight of them to reach full power. It is possible to run on only six cylinders, but it's not healthy. Nor is it the way the car was designed. People constantly learn to live with worry, fear, and other emotional pressures all the time and end up thinking their "motor" is running fine. The problem is that they've learned to define what is normal by their sub-normal lifestyle. Holding on to resentment and the like actually drains power from our engine and disqualifies us from significant spiritual breakthrough. Repentance is the beginning of the answer. It brings us into forgiveness and into our purpose.

HUNDRED-YEAR VISION

We believe God has required us to have a 100-year vision for our church. In other words, we constantly make decisions with the knowledge they will affect a generation that we will never see. "*A good man leaves an inheritance to his children's children*" (Prov. 13:22). God's righteousness makes us good. And it's His righteousness that causes us to see the effect of our decisions today on the generations that follow.

This vision is possible only through the discovery of divine purpose. As we see the eternal purpose of God for His people, we are able to develop lifestyles that are consistent with such a purpose. The end result is that we make His purposes perceivable to the unbeliever.

We are first and foremost a people of God's presence. The Church is the eternal dwelling place of God. As such we are known for our ministry *to God*, which positions and equips us for more effective ministry *to people*. For example, evangelism in its purist form is simply an overflow of worship. If the glory of God could be seen on and within the house(s) of God in the Old Testament—though the hands of man built them—how much more is that glory witnessed in this house called the church; for God is building His Church (see Matt. 16:18).

We are to display the wisdom of God to be seen by all those in positions of power—including the principalities and powers in heavenly places. The creative expression that comes through wisdom is a reminder to all that exists that this company of believers is commissioned to bring heavenly answers to earthly problems. This will turn heads from the inferior wisdom of this world to the divine wisdom that answers the cry of the human heart.

As His delegated authority on earth we have the responsibility to carry on the assignment that Jesus received from the Father— "*...destroy the works of the devil*" (1 John 3:8). The devil is defeated, but many of his works remain unchallenged. Before Jesus was taken to Heaven, He passed on the same commission to us that His Father gave to Him (see John 20:21). This is the overt ministry style of addressing those parts of people's lives that have been affected by the one who came to "*kill, steal, and destroy*" (John 10:10).

MOUNTAINS TO MOVE

There are two basic mountains of opposition to the way of thinking that has us build for another generation to enjoy. The first is our own selfishness. It's easy to think in terms of what is best for us and lose sight of the ones that have to sleep in the bed we make. Hezekiah made such a mistake. He sinned by showing his complete treasury to foreigners. When the prophet rebuked him, he did so by saying, "'*Behold, the days are coming when all that is in your house, and all that your fathers have laid up in store to this day will be carried to Babylon; nothing shall be left,*' says the Lord. '*Some of your sons who*

— 165 —

shall issue from you, whom you will beget, will be taken away; and they will become officials in the palace of the king of Babylon'" (2 Kings 20:17-18 NASB). It's hard to imagine how such a great reformer could have fallen so far but his shocking response is as follows, *"'The word of the Lord which you have spoken is good.' For he thought, 'Is it not so, if there will be peace and truth in my days?'"* (2 Kings 20:19 NASB). It's sad to see how one so great thought solely about himself in a time when he learned his family line would bear a curse because of his foolish choice. He was actually so happy that he would enjoy blessing in his day that he lost sight of being the one leaving a legacy of evil for his descendants. He left them with a curse instead of a blessing, which is a stunning end to a great revivalist's life.

The second problem is it's difficult to have a 100-year vision for a planet you believe will soon burn because of God's judgment. It's hard to occupy, as we were commanded, and pray for His dominion to be demonstrated when our hope is based entirely on life in Heaven. This is a difficult tension for the church that exists between supposedly conflicting truths; our *blessed hope* in Christ' return, and our delight in the privilege of praying and laboring for His Kingdom (the King's Dominion) to come—now! The promise of Christ's return does not give me permission to be irresponsible with Christ's command.

SHEEP AND GOAT NATIONS

We have the honor of living at a time when our lives make a dramatic difference in the outcome of world events. We were born for this hour. Our assignment is to live as though nothing were impossible. The command to disciple nations is not figurative. It was a literal command that has the backing of Heaven for those who embrace the assignment. This is a time when "sheep" and "goat" nations are being decided. Silence by the church, or unbelief concerning divine purpose, can cost us the privilege of fulfilling that part of our commission. It will end in disaster for many nations that could have had a significant outpouring of the Spirit.

Regardless of how and when you believe we are going to be taken to Heaven, we must rid ourselves of the idea that Jesus is coming to *rescue* His church. That lie has dislocated many generations of revolutionaries from their purpose in the same way a joint is pulled out of place. It has put the Church into a defensive posture of occupation to protect what we have instead of positioning ourselves for the purpose of increase. The strategy of occupation for the purpose of advancement and increase is an absolute Kingdom principle. Ask the man who buried his talent in order to protect it (see Matt. 25:24-28). He occupied (possessed) to protect (preserve) without increasing what he was given and suffered eternal consequences for his choice.

The Ultimate Challenge in Stewardship

This takes us to our final truth for this challenge. We have been given the opportunity to shape the course of world history by learning to bring into our day, things that were reserved for another day. That is the subject of the last chapter.

ENDNOTES

1. We found this to be a primary truth in raising our children. Disciplining for right attitudes prevents a lot of heartbreak in wrong actions. But the parents must model this principle first.

2. Remember, Kingdom abundance is not measured in what I have, but what I've given away.

CHAPTER 10

Pulling Tomorrow Into Today

We own in the present what is not yet.

To resource the earth with Heaven's resources, our under-standing of stewardship must grow. Many struggle when-ever leaders teach about our simple role stewarding money, and automatically disqualify themselves from the weightier issues—like responsibly managing our gifts, time, relationships, and the world we live in. But the greatest honor bestowed on us as stewards is the responsibility to steward tomorrow, today.

Our role in shaping the world around us through creative expression is never more at the forefront than when we joyfully learn to pull tomorrow into today. God trains us for this role when-ever He speaks to us, for in doing so He is working to awaken and establish our affections for His Kingdom. A people whose hearts are anchored in His world are best qualified to serve in this one. He establishes His eternal purpose in us whenever He speaks. His Word comes from eternity into time, giving us a track to ride on. It con-nects us with eternity, causing us to impact our world through the influence of His world.

INHERITANCE 101

The believer's inheritance is beyond human comprehension. To put the richness of that gift into the eternal future is to sell short the power of the Cross in the present. He gave us a gift beyond comprehension because we have an assignment beyond reason. Jesus gave us all things because we would need *all things* to fulfill our call. He intends to fill the earth with His glory, and His glorious Bride will play a role.

It is interesting to note that we have already inherited tomorrow— *things to come*. That makes us stewards of tomorrow in a profound way. God reveals coming events to us, and we steward the timing of those events. This amazing privilege is exemplified in Scripture and gives insight to passages that might otherwise be hard to understand.

ISRAEL WAS BLINDED BY GOD

Many times throughout the Scriptures we are faced with statements and principles that challenge our understanding of God. It's never that He could be perceived as evil or untrustworthy; but He is often mysterious and unpredictable.

Such a case is found in the Gospel of John. At first glance it looks as though God has it in for Israel and that He hopes they don't repent because He doesn't want to heal them.

He has blinded their eyes and He hardened their heart, so that they would not see with their eyes and perceive with their heart, and be converted and I should heal them (John 12:40 NASB).

Yet the whole of Scripture gives us a different picture. We know God never hardens a tender heart. It's the tender heart that receives what God is saying and doing. Wherever people have truly sought God, He has welcomed them with much mercy and grace, as He is the restorer of broken lives. But a hard heart is a different story completely, as God will harden a hard heart.

Pharaoh is probably the best example of this (see Exod. 7). The Bible says that he hardened his heart against the Lord, and did so repeatedly. So God finally hardened his heart for him, making his condition permanent. If Pharaoh would not be used as an instrument of righteousness, then God would use his evil to display His wonders. God's intent was now to use him as a "chess piece" for His purposes.

Israel was similarly hardened and used for His purposes. They had watched Jesus' ministry firsthand for over three years. While Nazareth was the only city we know of to resist because of unbelief, the others still didn't repent even though they saw extraordinary miracles (see Matt. 11:21). Seeing God display His wonders has a price tag—we can no longer live (think and act) the same way we did before. Miracles display God's dominion with a clarity that is seldom seen in the rest of life. To see and not change is to bring judgment upon ourselves. Such was the case for many of the cities of Israel.

God is perfect in wisdom, and is able to use the worst that man can dish out for His glory. In His sovereignty, He chose to use this *season of rejection of the Gospel* as the time He would add the Gentiles to the faith. This is discussed more clearly in Romans 11:

> *I say then, have they stumbled that they should fall? Certainly not! But through their fall, to provoke them to jealousy, salvation has come to the Gentiles* (Romans 11:11).

Israel's rejection of Jesus provided the opportunity for the Gentiles to be grafted into the olive tree, the *Israel of God* (Gal. 6:16; Rom. 11:17-24). The entire story is a fascinating study about God's sovereign plan to save people from every tribe, tongue, and nation, but unpacking this is not the purpose of this chapter. Rather, tucked away in this wonderful story is a remarkable truth: if Israel would have seen what God had purposed for them within His Kingdom in the last days, and asked for it, God would have had to give it to them. He would have answered them even though it was not His correct time for that promise to be fulfilled. So He used their hardness of heart as the basis for blinding them to insure that His purposes would be accomplished on His timetable. Instead of just saying "No," He responded by hardening their already hard hearts so they would lose their ability to perceive Kingdom possibilities.

The implication of the story—if you see it, you can have it! Perhaps it would be better to say, if God lets you see future promises, it's because He's hoping they will hook you, and cause you to hunger for those things. It is through a desperate heart that you are able to bring the fulfillment of those promises into your day.

THE PURPOSE OF REVELATION

Revelation means "to lift the veil." It is to remove a cover over something so we can see it more clearly. It doesn't create something; it simply reveals what was already there. When God reveals coming events and promises, He is giving us access to a realm in Him. All of the promises He reveals to us will be realized in time, but the acceleration of events is largely determined by the desperation of God's people. Our passion for Him and His promises speeds up the process of growth and development, making us qualified for the stewardship of those events sooner than had been planned.

BIBLICAL PRECEDENTS

Jesus and His mother, Mary, went to a wedding in John chapter 2. After they were there for a while, Mary noticed the wedding party was out of wine. She spoke to Jesus about their problem. Jesus' responded, "*Woman, what does that have to do with us? My hour has not yet come*" (John 2:4 NASB). Since Jesus only said and did what He picked up from His Father (see John 5:19), He let her know that this was not the right time to reveal Him as the miracle worker. Mary had been *pregnant* with God's promises about her son for 30 years, and found it difficult to wait much longer. She turned to the servants and told them to do whatever Jesus said. Jesus, who got all His direction from His heavenly Father, now perceived that this had become the right time. Amazing! God's timing changed! What was reserved for another day (revealing Jesus as the miracle worker) was pulled into her day through her desperation.

Another time, Jesus ministered to a woman at the well. She was a Samaritan. Jesus so profoundly impacted her that she was able to persuade the entire city to come and hear Him speak. They believed at first because of the woman's testimony, but ended up believing out of their personal contact with Him. What is important to remember is that this was not supposed to be the time for the non-Jews to hear the Gospel. The disciples were not even allowed the chance to preach to them when they were commissioned in Matthew 10 as that new focus would come after the death and resurrection of Jesus. Yet in this story, the people of the city begged Jesus to stay two more days, which He did. They pulled a privilege into their day that was reserved for another time.

THE MOST PROFOUND STORY

King David takes the prize for having perhaps the greatest story which illustrates this principle. His situation is hard for us to imagine—he was under the law. Only the high priest could come before the actual presence of God. His presence dwelt upon the mercy seat, which was inside the Holy of Holies. He could only come bringing a basin of blood, hoping that God would indeed accept the sacrifice and postpone the penalty of sin for one more year. If anyone other than the priest ever came into God's actual presence, they would die. God would kill them. There certainly wasn't a careless attitude about going to church in those days.

David is known as the man after God's heart. He had a revelation of changes in their approach to God, confirmed by Nathan and Gad, the prophets who served in his court. This insight changed everything. He saw that the blood of bulls and goats did nothing to really touch the heart of God, and that He was really looking for the sacrifices of brokenness and contrition. Another radical change that would have been nearly unimaginable in that day was that every priest would be welcome into God's presence daily. And they didn't come with a basin of blood, but instead came offering sacrifices of thanksgiving and praise.

Preparations began. The musicians and singers were trained. Israel was getting herself ready for the presence of God to return to Jerusalem. Saul, Israel's former king, had little regard for the ark of the covenant.[1] But David wanted God's presence more than anything. While there were initial problems, due to the fact they did not follow God's instructions for carrying the Ark of the Covenant, David eventually got his wish. He pitched a tent for the Ark and with great celebration brought His presence into the city and placed it into the tent. According to David's directions, the priests ministered to God 24 hours a day, for decades. There were no sacrifices of animals before His presence in this tent. It was 100 percent worship.

It's important to note two things: One, what they did was forbidden by the law they lived under. And two, they were given a sneak preview of New Testament church life. Because of the blood of Jesus, each believer has access to the presence of God to minister to Him with thanksgiving, praise, and worship.

David was primarily a worshiper. As a young man he no doubt learned much about the presence and heart of God. He tasted of a lifestyle that was reserved for New Testament believers, yet hungered for that in his day. His hunger for what he saw became so strong that God let him have something in his day that was reserved for another day.

CROSSING THE GREAT DIVIDE

We have a bad habit of taking most of the good promises of the Bible and sweeping them under the mysterious rug we call "the millennium." It is a great inconsistency to say the last days began with the day of Pentecost with Acts 2, and then take the wonderful promises of the prophets about the last days and say they refer to the millennium. For example, Micah 4:1-2 (NASB) says, "*And it will come about in the last days…Many nations will come and say, 'Come and let us go up to the mountain of the Lord and to the house of the God of Jacob, that He may teach us about His ways and that we may walk in His paths….'*" The error of our ways is clearly realized in the fact that what is believed actually requires little or no faith to get what most of the Church is waiting for—the world to get worse, and the Church to get rescued. This is an irresponsible way to respond to great promise.

Had David lived with such a mind-set, he would have had to live under the restraint of Old Testament law, and not provide us the testimony of a life of celebration and joy. He illustrated the New Testament believer before there ever was such a thing.

If ever there was a line to cross where it should have been impossible to bring something from a future era into a given time, it should have been during David's day. The barrier between the law and grace was so large that what David did would have been impossible to predict, were we on the other side of the Cross. Yet the desperation of a hungry heart brought about the impossible. It drew into their hour something that was not just for the future. Nor was it just reserved for another day; it was for another race of people.[2] Yet David brought this greatest of life's privileges across the greatest divide imaginable. He had daily access to the glory of His presence! This would be something that only the blood of Jesus could make possible.

Our Greatest Challenge

If it's true that the promises of restored cities and healed nations are actually millennium promises…and if the promise of God's glory being manifest all over the earth is far off into the future…and if in fact the people of God will not reach a place of true maturity, living like one mature man—then I must ask these questions: Is there anyone hungry enough for what He has shown us in the Scriptures that we will pull into our day something that is reserved for another? Is there anyone willing to lay themselves down to bring more of God's promises across another great divide? Or how about the promise that says everyone will know the Lord? (See Jer. 31:34.) Isn't that one worth pursuing for our cities?

If what I have shared is true, then no one can hide behind their eschatology. No one is exempt because of the doctrinal interpretation of the last days. No one is excused. If you can see the coming future promises, and He hasn't blinded your eyes to His intent, then He is hoping to hook you into the role of calling "*into being that which does not exist*" (Rom. 4:17 NASB). It is the role of the desperate heart of faith. We have the opportunity to affect the direction and flow of history through our prayers and intercessions. This is when we take hold of the future. This is why He wants to show us, "*things to come*" (John 16:13). The future is now, and it belongs to us.

WHERE DID ALL THE SEASONS GO

His Kingdom only knows increase and acceleration. It is the hunger of God's people that helps accelerate the process of development and growth, and actually speeds up time. It is my conviction that God is trying to get rid of our excuse concerning "seasons." Many have lived in a spiritual winter for most of their lives and called it *God's dealings*. The metaphor of the seasons has become an excuse for moodiness, unbelief, depression, inactivity, and the like. It must end. As the technological development has increased exponentially, so the development and maturity of this generation will increase.

Trees planted by God's river bear fruit 12 months of the year. They are the prophetic prototype of the last days' generation that has experienced the acceleration prophesied. How else do you think it's possible for the *"plowman to overtake the reaper?"* (Amos 9:13). This is an amazing prophetic picture of a time when planting and harvesting are done in one motion. How else can we come into the maturity talked about in Zechariah when the weakest among us is like David and the strongest is like God? (See Zech. 12:8.) These things are reserved for the hour directly ahead of us. Let's grab hold of tomorrow, today. We don't have time to waste and then blame God for it. It is the season to apprehend, because we see!

There's a message for us in the cursed fig tree. Jesus cursed it for not bearing fruit *out of season*. It died immediately. Was He unreasonable? Did He lose His temper? Or was He showing us something about His expectations for our lives that we'd just as soon ignore? He has the right to expect the fruit of the impossible from those He has created for the impossible. The Spirit of the resurrected Christ living in me has disqualified me from the mundane and ordinary. I am qualified for the impossible, because I'm a believing believer. Faith qualifies me for the impossible.

We have a plant in our prayer house that is supposed to have blossoms for a couple months of the year. But in the presence of the Lord upon that prayer house, it blooms year-round. He is trying to get our attention with natural phenomenon that point to these truths.

It's New Day

God is using the hunger of His people to increase the momentum of the day, bringing about drastic changes in the pace of development. Brand-new believers are not waiting for the *mature* to tell them that something is possible. They've read the Book, and they know it's legal. This tattooed generation with their body piercings and little fear of death has locked into the possibility of significance. They have seen what prior generations have called impossible, and will settle for nothing less. I, for one, join myself with them in the quest for the authentic Gospel that has no walls, no impossibilities, with an absolute surrender to the King and His Kingdom.

God doesn't reveal coming events to make us strategists. He shows us the future to make us dissatisfied[3] because hungry people move the resources of Heaven like no one else possibly could. It's the real reason the rich have such a hard time entering the Kingdom—there's so little hunger for what is real, what is unseen—their desperation has been numbed by an abundance of the inferior.

THE PURPOSE OF CONTENDING

Two years ago I sought for a breakthrough in my dad's healing. It never came, and he went home to be with Jesus—but that's a story for another day. Let's just say there are no deficiencies on God's side of the equation. It felt like I was pushing against a 1,000-pound rock that wouldn't budge. And although I pushed against that rock for months, it never moved. We celebrated his home-going and vowed to continue to push against those things which cut people's lives short.

It wasn't too long afterward that I realized that while I never moved that 1,000-pound boulder, I can now move the 500-pound rock right next to it. And I couldn't have moved this size rock before contending with the 1,000-pounder. Contending shapes us and makes us capable of carrying more than we've ever been able before, and opens up for us areas of anointing in ministry that were previously out of reach.

Often times God uses the fight to increase a person's experience in Him, far above all those around them. I call it *a spike in human experience.* In times past, people with that elevated position of experience and the extraordinary anointing and favor that goes with it, used it to draw people to themselves to receive from their gift. While that is always a part of the purpose of a gift, it falls short of God's intent entirely. The elevated experience is the position to equip the Body of Christ so that what was once the high point of breakthrough for an individual has become the new norm for the Church. Contending brings a breakthrough that must be shared. All must benefit from the price we pay to labor through the heat of the day. It's just His way.

DREAMERS, LET'S GATHER

We are in a race. It's a race between what is and what could be. We are uniquely positioned with the richest inheritance of all time. It has been accumulating through several thousand years of humanity encountering God, and God encountering humanity. The righteous dead are watching. They fill the heavenly stands, and have been given the name, *"cloud of witnesses"* (Heb. 12:1). They realize that in a relay race, each runner receives a prize according to how the last runner finishes. They invested in us for this final leg of the race, and are now waiting to see what we will do with what we've been given.

We've been given the capacity to dream and, more importantly, to dream with God. His language continues to be unveiled, His heart is being imparted, and permission has been given to try to exaggerate His goodness. We have been given the right to surpass the accomplishments of previous generations using creativity through wisdom to solve the issues facing us. Their ceiling is our floor. This is our time to run.

ONLY CHILDREN ARE READY

I remember when I was a child and my parents would have guests come over to our house to visit. It was always exciting to be part of the food and the fun. But it was painful to have to go to bed while they were still there, sitting in our living room, talking and having fun. The laughter that echoed back into my room was just torture. It was impossible for me to sleep in that atmosphere. Sometimes, when I couldn't take it any longer, I would sneak quietly into the hallway, just to listen. I didn't want to miss anything. If my parents caught me they usually sent me back to bed. But there were a few times when they thought my curiosity was humorous enough to let me come out to be with them just a little longer. The risk was worth it!

I'm in the hallway again. And the thought of missing something that could have been the experience of my generation is pure torture. I can't possibly sleep in this atmosphere, because if I do, I know I'll miss the reason for which I was born.

ENDNOTES

1. A gold-covered box, with the Mercy Seat on top—this is where the Presence of God dwelt for Israel.

2. Believers are actually a new creation, a new race of people. See 2 Corinthians 5:17 and 1 Peter 2:9.

3. One of the secrets of maintaining a revival is being thankful for what God has done, while remaining dissatisfied because there is more.

Contact Information and Resources

Bill Johnson
Bethel Church
933 College View Drive
Redding, CA 96003

www.BillJohnsonMinistries.com

www.iBethel.org

Resources

Revolution:
Erasing the Lines Between the Secular and the Sacred
Single CD

When the believer comes into the Kingdom, there is no such thing as a secular part of their life; everything becomes purposeful. God is leveling the playing field of the Kingdom, where businesspeople, schoolteachers, wives and mothers—the "ministers of the Gospel"—live with significance, shaping the course of worldwide history. By giving a complete "Yes" to God, they step into a role of living on the edge of what God is doing, making it the center of what is to come.

www.BillJohnsonMinistries.com
www.iBethel.org

Healing:
Our Neglected Birthright
6 CD Set

Any area of a person's life that is not under the influence of hope is under the influence of a lie. Hope is the atmosphere in which faith grows. It is natural for a Christian to hunger to see the impossibilities of people bow at the name of Jesus because we are a people born to confront and reverse the works of the devil. This series is a practical tool of discovering the full provision of the Cross and how Jesus has enabled us to be successful in fulfilling His mandate.

www.BillJohnsonMinistries.com
www.iBethel.org

The Advancing Kingdom:
A Practical Guide to the Normal Christian
Life of Victory and Purpose
4 CD Set

The strategies of hell are to distract and derail us from God's agenda through accusations and intimidation. The safest place for the believer is not in defending what we have, but in positioning ourselves for advancement. It's the sacrificial lifestyle that creates an atmosphere around the believer that insulates us from the destructive tactics of the devil and enables us to walk in increasing victory and joy.

www.BillJohnsonMinistries.com
www.iBethel.org

Leading From the Heart
8 CD Set

God has raised up true leaders the same way for centuries with training that begins with the heart. Skills can be learned, but a Christ-like heart comes through repentance, discipline, and encounters with God Himself. Our faithfulness in these areas determines how much authority we can be trusted with. This series addresses the multifaceted characteristics of a leader who walks in loyalty, grace, wisdom and most importantly, with a value above all for the presence of God.

www.BillJohnsonMinistries.com
www.iBethel.org

The Quest:
For the Face of God
4 CD Set

Our initial response to God is our salvation, yet the "Quest" lies within our ultimate response of seeking and experiencing His face. He is the center. As we experience the Face of God, that outpouring brings a new identity of influence and favor that empowers us to change the course of history. Join the quest. It is all consuming and glorious beyond description.

www.BillJohnsonMinistries.com
www.iBethel.org

From Glory To Glory:
Biblical Patterns for Sustaining Revival
4 CD Set

Every believer has the responsibility to carry revival as if they are the only one responsible. God's manifest presence and favor marked the Church of Acts with uncompromising standards, which caused the message of the Church to increase in its power and demonstration. This message illustrates how Kingdom increase is the calculated devotion to a move of God; exposing some of the tests that prove our readiness for more and how we capture the favor and attention of Heaven through a lifestyle of faithfulness and honor.

www.BillJohnsonMinistries.com
www.iBethel.org

Coming Pentecost:
Position Yourself
2 CD Set

The historic outpourings of God have fueled the heart cry for Him to do it again in our day, unaware that underneath the dry soil of our present circumstances is the rain from the last outpouring. We wait for just one more touch so we can come into our destiny, not knowing we are positioned for our greatest victory. Be challenged to "get up now" and allow God to shine on you, as you position yourself and steward the "more" you have prayed for.

www.BillJohnsonMinistries.com
www.iBethel.org

Dreaming with God:
Unveiling the Mystery of Co-laboring with Christ
4 CD Set

Much of the Church is waiting for a command from the Lord while He is waiting for the dream of His people. We have yet to learn the radical difference between being a task-oriented servant of God versus being a friend. God is restoring the Church to the creative role that is receptive to God through vulnerability, and opens us up to His world of possibilities. God is transforming our minds to the full expression of being a co-laborer with Christ, so that our will can be done.

www.BillJohnsonMinistries.com
www.iBethel.org